The Kimbell
COOKBOOK

Kimbell Art Museum
. . . serving the Fort Worth/Dallas metropolitan community

First Printing 5,000 copies 1986
Second Printing 5,000 copies 1988
Library of Congress Catalog Card No. 86-080903
ISBN Number 0-912804-23-8

On the cover:
Luis Meléndez, Spanish, 1716-1780,
Still Life with Oranges, Jars, and Boxes of Sweets,
ca. 1760-65, oil on canvas

Additional copies may be obtained by addressing:

The Kimbell Cookbook
Kimbell Art Museum
3333 Camp Bowie Boulevard
Fort Worth, Texas 76107

Printed by Hart Graphics, Inc.
Austin, Texas

FOREWORD

Since its opening in 1972, the Kimbell Art Museum has won great acclaim for its classic modern building. Over the same period, its collections have grown dramatically in scope and quality. Both of these factors have contributed to the current reputation of the gallery as possibly "the finest small museum in the country."

Kay Kimbell—a successful entrepreneur in the grain business, retailing, real estate, and petroleum—established the Kimbell Art Foundation in the 1930s, shortly after making his first purchases of paintings. When Mr. Kimbell died in 1964, his collection numbered several hundred paintings, all of which he left to the Foundation, whose sole purpose was to create and operate in Fort Worth a public museum of the first order.

The well-known Philadelphia architect, the late Louis I. Kahn, designed and supervised the construction of the Kimbell Art Museum between 1967 and 1972. The last building completed during the architect's lifetime, the Museum is considered his finest creation. The building's gracious proportions, fine craftsmanship, natural light, and beautiful landscaping, all combine to lend the structure a sense of serenity and restraint.

Conceived from the beginning as a small museum of high-quality objects ranging over the entire history of art—Eastern and Western—the Kimbell's collection now numbers around 600 objects. These include an outstanding group of Far Eastern objects from pre-historic times to the nineteenth century, a select group of Pre-Columbian works, a small selection of African objects, prints and drawings, and Mediterranean antiquities. The collection's greatest strength, however, lies in its representation of the development of European painting from the Renaissance to the early twentieth century. Outstanding examples can be found by Duccio, Fra Angelico, Bellini, Holbein, Tintoretto, Annibale Carracci, El Greco, Georges de La Tour, Le Nain, Poussin, Claude Lorrain, Rembrandt, Rubens, Ribera, Velázquez, Murillo, Pietro da Cortona, Tiepolo, Watteau, Chardin, Boucher, Greuze, Gainsborough, Stubbs, Goya, David, Corot, Delacroix, Courbet, Turner, Friedrich, Monet, Manet, Pissaro, Caillebotte, Cézanne, Picasso, Mondrian, Munch, Mirò, Matisse, and many others. Complementing the permanent collection is a full schedule of temporary exhibitions, many of them organized by the Museum, and an active program of lectures, films, and special events.

PREFACE

The Kimbell Art Museum decided in 1981 to expand its modest snack bar into a full-service buffet restaurant providing daily luncheon and afternoon refreshments to museum visitors. I was managing a small catering business at the time. Lacking any formal training in restaurant management, I conceived of a menu limited to soups, salads, and desserts; it wasn't long before out-of-town visitors as well as local patrons began to frequent the Kimbell for lunch, as well as for "cultural" nourishment in the adjoining galleries. The architectural ambience is unique, and the service has grown to include espresso, cappuccino, and many specialty items, as well as a selection of beers and wines, both domestic and imported. On Sundays quiche, sandwiches and other light fare are served, as well as soup and salad.

This book was a natural consequence of the requests from patrons for copies of my recipes. After two years of testing, tasting, writing, and rewriting, I felt that I was ready to present my favorite and most popular appetizers, soups, salads, and desserts in the form of a cookbook. *The Kimbell Cookbook* is the result of my efforts to develop and refine recipes especially suited to the tastes of a broad museum audience.

I would like to express my sincere gratitude to those whose assistance contributed to its creation: The Buffet staff, many of whom donated, tasted, and edited the recipes; the various members of the Museum staff who helped to assemble the recipes for publication; Renie Steves and Louise Lamensdorf, whose classes at the French Apron School of Cooking, with their special blend of classical and modern cuisines, stimulated my imagination; the authors of all the culinary publications whose pages provided new concepts for me; all of my friends for their recipes and encouragement; and my super family who may never be able to face another bowl of soup.

Shelby Volk
Buffet Manager

MENUS

Sausage and Clam Soup
Pasta Salad
Italian Cream Cake

Pot Luck Chili
Mushroom Cheese Salad
Pecan Pie

Red Beans and Rice Soup
Marinated Vegetables
Sweet Potato Pie

MENUS

Cream of Cauliflower Soup
Snow Pea Salad
Lemon Pie with Sauce Cardinale

Cream of Chicken with Cheese Soup
Pea Salad
Chocolate Zucchini Cake

Cream of Artichoke Soup
White Bean and Tuna Salad
Raisin Pecan Pie

MENUS

Pasta and Bean Soup
Fresh Tomato and Mozzarella Salad
Lemon Pound Cake with Blueberry Sauce

Black Bean Soup
Egg Salad
Rum Cake

Blackeyed Pea Soup
Smoked Turkey Salad
Swedish Apple Nut Pie

MENUS

Curried Zucchini Soup
Chicken Salad
Blueberry Pie with Whipped Cream

Gazpacho
Rice Salad
Pineapple Cream Cheese Pie

Avocado Soup
Sesame Chicken Salad
Peach Pie

MENUS

Broccoli Soup
Macaroni Salad
Anna's Chocolate Cake

Senegalese
French Apron Pâté Salad
Lemon Almond Squares

Cream of Pimiento Soup
Scallop Salad
Apple Pie

Egyptian, XIX Dynasty, ca. 1320-1200 B.C.,
Ramesses II, from the Temple of Mut
at Karnak, granite

SOUPS

I have always loved to experiment — from mudpies in the backyard to chemistry in college. I love to make soups because there is considerable latitude for experimenting. I am never content to use just one recipe for anything. My collection of some forty to fifty cookbooks is well worn. In this spirit, I have made suggestions for substitutions throughout the recipes published here. Use them and expand upon them to suit your own tastes.

Remember that your final product will only be as good as the ingredients that you use to make it. (The emphasis in cooking today is on fresh ingredients. Consequently, the quality of produce available has greatly improved.) However, because of the quantity needed for The Buffet, I sometimes rely on certain canned or frozen ingredients, that occasionally appear in the recipes presented here. For example, we use a lot of canned tomatoes. The reason is twofold: first, the amount of labor necessary to peel, seed and chop that many tomatoes is excessive and, secondly, good, fresh tomatoes are not always available.

We have found that processed cheeses lend themselves better to soups because they do not fall apart into a greasy rubbery mass when heated. If fresh cheese is used, add it quickly at the last. Fresh Parmesan is great as a garnish for soup and salad; toss out those cans of Parmesan.

I have used dried herbs in these recipes unless otherwise specified. If fresh herbs are readily available, the ratio to dried herbs is 3 to 1.

When seasoning soups, remember that many ingredients such as bouillon cubes, stock bases, cheeses, ham and sausage, already contain salt. Further, flavor increases as the liquid cooks away. Therefore, you should always taste before adding salt and pepper.

We hope these recipes will increase your interest in cooking by sparking your imagination and providing some fun when you are going through the mental gymnastics of "what to have for dinner."

French Apron Chicken Stock

Put chicken and all parts, except liver, in a large stock pot with cold water. Bring to a boil, skimming off froth as it rises to the top. Add remaining ingredients. Allow to cook at a gentle simmer for an hour. Remove whole chicken and allow to cool. Remove meat, reserving for another use, and return bones to pot. Continue to simmer for another 2 to 4 hours. Let bones cool in the stock for an hour or so. Strain and refrigerate in 2 or 3 small containers so that stock cools quickly. Remove fat from top of cooled stock. Now the stock is ready to use. To reduce the stock for freezing, simmer over low heat until it becomes dark and sticky. Pour into a pyrex dish to cool. Cut into cubes and freeze. Then thaw and add water to create desired strength.

I really like to make stock. It's getting down to basics. Good, rich stock is essential to making good sauces and soups. I confess that we use Sexton's chicken, beef and ham base. They work quite well in soups but not so well in any reduction-type sauce because they are rather salty.

1	*(2½-3) pound chicken, plus a package of wings or backs*
16	*cups water*
2	*carrots*
1	*leek*
1	*onion stuck with 2 cloves*
1	*garlic clove*
2	*stalks celery with leaves*
1	*bay leaf*
	A few parsley sprigs
½	*teaspoon thyme*
8	*peppercorns, slightly crushed*

French Apron Beef Stock

3	*pounds beef bones*
2½	*pounds chicken wings and backs*
2½	*pounds veal bones*
1	*large carrot, cut into chunks*
1	*large onion, coarsely chopped*

Call the butcher before you make the trip to be sure he has the bones. If you can't get veal bones, beef will do. Or if you don't find leeks anywhere, use a little extra onion.

In a large roasting pan, or 2 smaller ones, brown bones including chicken wings and backs at 425° for 45 to 50 minutes, stirring and turning once or twice. Add carrot and continue browning for another 15 to 20 minutes. Add onion, browning for 15 to 20 minutes more. Everything should be *very* brown. Transfer bones and vegetables to a large stock pot. Drain excess fat from roasting pan. Over medium high heat, deglaze pan with one cup water, stirring to catch all the brown goody on the bottom and sides of the pan. Add this to stock pot along with 9 quarts water. Bring to a boil, reduce heat and simmer for an hour, skimming the froth as it rises.

2	*large onions, each stuck with 2 cloves*
2	*large carrots*
1	*leek, coarsely chopped*
3	*ribs celery with leaves*
1	*garlic clove*
	A few parsley sprigs
3	*tomatoes, cut in quarters*
1	*bay leaf*
½	*teaspoon thyme*
1	*teaspoon peppercorns, slightly crushed*

Add all remaining vegetables and seasonings to stock pot. Continue to simmer very slowly for 8 to 10 hours, adding more water as necessary to maintain original water level. Cool broth and strain. Refrigerate. Remove fat from top. Now the stock is ready for use.

To make demi-glace, measure out a specified number of cups of stock and reduce it slowly to one third of the original volume.

To make glace de viande (meat glaze), reduce stock over low heat from 4 cups to ½ cup. The mixture will become dark brown and form bubbles on top like caramel during the last 15 to 20 minutes of cooking. Pour into a pyrex dish to cool. Cut into cubes and freeze.

These small portions are easier to store in the freezer. To use demi-glace or glace de viande for soups or sauce, just add enough water to achieve the desired strength.

French Apron Brown Veal Stock

Brown bones in a large roasting pan, or two smaller ones, at 475° for one hour, turning occasionally to brown on all sides. Add carrots and brown for another 15 to 20 minutes. Add onions and leek, continuing to brown for another 15 to 20 minutes. Transfer bones and vegetables from pan to stock pot. Drain off excess fat. Deglaze pan over medium heat with white wine, scraping bottom and sides of pan to get all the brown goody, and add to stock pot. Add 9 quarts water to pot. Bring to a boil slowly. Turn down heat and simmer for 1 hour, skimming to remove froth as it accumulates.

8-10 *pounds veal bones, skin and marrow*
2 *large carrots, cut in 2 inch slices*
2 *large onions, quartered*
1 *large leek*
2 *cups white wine*
9 *quarts water*

Add above vegetables after the first hour and continue to cook very slowly for about 24 hours. Occasionally add water to maintain the original water level. Cool stock with bones and vegetables in it. Strain and refrigerate. Remove fat from top and the stock is ready to use.

To make demi-glace, measure out a specified number of cups of stock, after removing fat, and reduce it slowly to one third the original volume.

To make glace de viande (meat glaze), reduce stock, on low heat, from 4 cups to ½ cup. The mixture will become dark brown and form bubbles on top like caramel during the last 15 to 20 minutes of cooking. Pour into pyrex dish to cool. Cut into cubes and store in freezer.

2 *large onions, stuck with 2 cloves*
2 *bay leaves*
½ *teaspoon black peppercorns, slightly crushed*
½ *teaspoon thyme*
4 *ribs celery*
1 *leek, coarsely chopped*
2 *garlic cloves*
A few parsley stems
2 *tomatoes cut in half*

21

French Apron Lean Fish Stock

2-3	*pounds fish trimmings (heads, tails and bones of cod, flounder, haddock, perch, pike, snapper, sole or swordfish)*
1	*teaspoon cardamon*
3	*whole cloves*
2	*unpeeled, medium onions, chopped*
2	*unpeeled garlic cloves*
1	*large carrot, coarsely chopped*
1	*bay leaf*
¼	*teaspoon each coriander and black peppercorns*
¼	*teaspoon each basil and marjoram*
1	*cup dry white wine*

In a pinch when fish stock is required, you may use bottled clam juice, but it can't hold a candle to this wonderful stock. Combine all ingredients except wine and water in a heavy stock pot. Cook over medium heat, stirring frequently, until fish trimmings exude juice, about 10 minutes. A small amount of water may be necessary to keep bones from sticking. Add wine and enough water to cover by about 2 inches. Bring to a simmer over medium heat, skimming off foam as it rises to the surface. Cover partially and simmer for 45 minutes. Taste stock. If more intense flavor is desired, continue to simmer. Cool. Strain into container and refrigerate until ready to use. May be refrigerated for a day or 2. May be frozen up to 2 months.

Yield: 5-6 cups

Onion Soup

There are two secrets to making outstanding onion soup: cooking the onions slowly over low heat and using a hearty beef stock. I think that a bowl of onion soup topped with lots of cheese, accompanied by green salad, crusty French bread and a bottle of red wine makes a wonderful winter supper.

Cook the onions in ¼ cup butter over low heat, stirring frequently until they are golden brown. This will take about 30 minutes. Sprinkle with a little flour, and when this is well blended, gradually add the beef stock. Bring the soup to a boil, stirring constantly. Lower heat and simmer for 20 to 30 minutes. Add the wine at the last if you like and taste for seasoning.

Butter the bread and toast it under the broiler or in a hot skillet.

To serve the soup gratiné, put the soup in ovenproof bowls and add the toasted bread and Swiss cheese and broil until the cheese begins to brown.

Yield: 6 cups
Serves: 3-4

6	**cups thinly sliced onions**
¼	**cup butter**
2	**tablespoons butter for toast**
5	**cups beef stock**
½	**glass red or white wine (optional)**
	Six thick slices French bread
1½	**cups (6 ounces) grated Swiss cheese or a combination of Swiss and Parmesan**

23

Vegetable Soup

This is a good soup with which to experiment because you can easily substitute vegetables. If you're watching calories, eliminate the olive oil and simmer all the vegetables in the stock. Substitute green beans or chicken or shrimp for the white beans. If you want an Italian flavor, add some basil, oregano, Italian sausage and pasta.

2	tablespoons olive oil
½	cup chopped onion
½	cup sliced carrots
2	quarts chicken stock
1	cup potatoes, peeled and diced
1	cup tomato juice
1	(14 ounce) can diced tomatoes or 1 cup fresh tomatoes, peeled, seeded and chopped
1½	cups cooked white or red beans
½	cup chopped parsley
1	cup fresh or frozen cut corn
1	garlic clove, crushed
1½	cups sliced zucchini

In a soup kettle, sauté onion and carrots in olive oil for about 10 minutes. Add remaining ingredients and simmer until the vegetables are just tender, never mushy, about 20 minutes. Season with basil, thyme, tarragon, whatever sounds good. Garnish with Parmesan cheese and croutons.

Yield: 12 cups
Serves: 8

Potato Soup

Melt butter in a large soup kettle. Add onion and sauté until soft. Add flour and cook, stirring, for 3 or 4 minutes. Then remove from heat and slowly stir in the hot chicken stock. Add carrots and celery and simmer gently for about 10 minutes. Then add potatoes and continue simmering until vegetables are tender, for about 20 minutes. Add seasonings and finish off with cream. Omit the cream and add more stock if you want to eliminate some calories.

2	*tablespoons butter*
¾	*cup chopped onion*
2	*tablespoons flour*
5	*cups hot chicken stock*
1	*cup sliced carrots*
¾	*cup sliced celery*
4	*cups peeled and diced potatoes*
¼	*cup chopped parsley*
1	*teaspoon season salt*
1	*teaspoon dill (optional)*
¼	*teaspoon pepper*
1	*cup whipping cream or half and half*

Yield: 8 cups
Serves: 4-6

Cream of Broccoli with Rice

In a saucepan, sauté onion in butter until transparent. Add chicken stock, rice and cream and bring to a boil. Reduce heat to medium and simmer for 15 minutes. Add broccoli and continue cooking until broccoli is tender, about 10 minutes. Season to your taste. The juice of half a lemon helps sharpen the taste.

2	*tablespoons butter*
½	*cup chopped onion*
1	*quart chicken stock*
⅓	*cup raw rice*
3	*cups whipping cream*
4-5	*cups (1 bunch) chopped broccoli*
1	*teaspoon seasoning salt*
¼	*teaspoon pepper*
	Juice of ½ lemon

Yield: 8 cups
Serves: 4-6

Cream of Artichoke Soup

2	cups chicken stock
¾	cup chopped onion
¾	cup chopped celery
¾	cup sliced carrots
1	cup sliced mushrooms
¼	teaspoon thyme
1	bay leaf
½	teaspoon sweet paprika
1	garlic clove, mashed
1	(14 ounce) can artichoke hearts or bottoms, chopped, reserve liquid
1½	cups whipping cream
1	cup (4 ounces) grated Swiss cheese
	Salt and pepper

In a saucepan, simmer the first 9 ingredients for 20 to 30 minutes, until the vegetables are just tender. Add cream, artichokes and liquid and continue simmering for 5 to 10 minutes until hot. Finish with the cheese and taste for seasoning.

Yield: 6 cups
Serves: 3-4

Cream of Cabbage Soup

½	cup chopped onions
½	cup sliced carrots
½	cup sliced celery
¾	cup peeled and diced potatoes
1	cup chicken stock
2	cups milk
2	cups whipping cream
4	cups chopped cabbage
1	tablespoon chopped parsley
¼	teaspoon paprika
	Salt
	Grated cheese for garnish

In a large saucepan, simmer onion, carrots, celery and potatoes in chicken stock for 10 to 15 minutes. Add milk, cream and cabbage and bring to a simmer again for about 10 minutes, until vegetables are tender. Taste soup and add seasonings to your liking. Garnish with cheese if desired.

Yield: 6 cups
Serves: 3-4

Cream of Cauliflower Soup

The bacon is not essential to this recipe. If you wish to omit it, just simmer the vegetables in the chicken stock until almost tender. If you like bacon, fry it until crisp, then add the onion, celery and carrots and sauté them quickly. Add cauliflower and chicken stock and simmer until tender, about 15 minutes. Add cream and heat through. Stir in parsley and cheese; then taste for seasoning. A little nutmeg would be good too. Using half broccoli and half cauliflower adds a nice touch of color.

Yield: 6-7 cups
Serves: 4

¼ *cup diced salt pork or bacon (optional)*
1 *cup chopped onion*
1 *cup sliced celery*
1 *cup sliced carrots*
3 *cups cauliflower, cut into flowerettes*
3 *cups chicken stock*
2 *cups whipping cream*
1 *tablespoon chopped parsley*
2 *cups (8 ounces) grated American or Swiss process cheese*
  Dash seasoning salt and cayenne

27

Cream of Carrot and Rice Soup

You could really use most any vegetable you like in this recipe:
broccoli, cauliflower, zucchini, asparagus, celery, spinach, and so on.

2	**tablespoons butter**
2	**cups sliced carrots**
⅔	**cup chopped onion**
1	**quart chicken stock**
¼	**cup white rice**
2	**cups whipping cream**
½	**teaspoon dill**
¼	**cup chopped parsley**
	Salt and cayenne

Melt butter in a large saucepan over low heat. Add carrots and onion and cook for about 10 minutes. Add stock and rice and simmer until vegetables are tender, about 15 to 20 minutes. At this point you may allow the soup to cool and then purée the soup in a food processor if you like. Or just add the cream and dill and simmer until soup is hot. Add the parsley just prior to serving. Taste for salt and cayenne.

Yield: 6 cups
Serves: 3-4

Cream of Spinach Soup with Cheese

In a heavy soup pot, melt butter and sauté the onion and garlic for about 5 minutes over medium heat. Add flour and cook, stirring for another 5 minutes. With the pan off the heat, whisk in the chicken stock. Return to stove and stir in cream, half and half, nutmeg and pepper. Simmer gently for 10 minutes, stirring occasionally. Turn heat to low; add spinach and continue cooking for another 10 minutes. Stir in cheese and heat through. Add salt to your taste and serve topped with bacon.

Yield: 6-7 cups
Serves: 4

2	*tablespoons butter*
⅔	*cup chopped onion*
1	*garlic clove, mashed*
3	*tablespoons flour*
2	*cups chicken broth*
1	*cup whipping cream*
1	*cup half and half*
⅛	*teaspoon nutmeg*
¼	*teaspoon pepper*
1	*(10 ounce) package fresh spinach, picked over, washed well, chopped, and squeezed dry*
1	*cup (4 ounces) grated Cheddar cheese*
	Salt
	Bacon bits (optional garnish)

Cream of Corn Soup

2   cups fresh or frozen cut corn
2   strips of bacon, chopped
2   tablespoons finely chopped
     onion
2   tablespoons flour
2   cups milk
½   teaspoon season salt
½   teaspoon pepper
2   cups half and half

Process 1 cup of the corn. Fry bacon in a large saucepan. Drain off all but 2 tablespoons of the grease. Add onion to bacon and sauté until soft. Stir in flour and cook, stirring for 5 minutes to make roux. Remove roux from heat and slowly stir in milk. Return to heat and add corn and remaining ingredients. Bring to a simmer, stirring until the mixture is thick. Taste for salt.

Yield: 6 cups
Serves: 3-4

Cream of Lettuce Soup

In a large saucepan, sauté onion in butter over low heat. Wash lettuce and drain it. Remove cores, cut heads in half and slice. Combine lettuce, carrot, potato and chicken stock in saucepan and simmer for 20 to 25 minutes. Allow soup to cool. Strain liquid and return it to saucepan. Purée the vegetables in a food processor and add to liquid. Stir in remaining ingredients. Simmer for 5 minutes. For a chilled soup, cool to room temperature and refrigerate covered for at least 4 hours. Adjust seasoning and garnish with fresh chives.

Yield: 6-7 cups
Serves: 3-4

1	small onion, chopped
1	tablespoon unsalted butter
4	heads Boston lettuce (about 7 ounces each)
1	medium carrot, peeled and sliced
1	small potato, peeled and chopped
5	cups chicken stock
½-1	cup whipping cream
1	tablespoon lemon juice
½	teaspoon salt
¼	teaspoon grated white pepper
	Pinch nutmeg or mace
	Minced chives for garnish

Cream of Tomato Soup

After having tried three recipes for this soup, I finally came upon one which called for a bit of baking soda, the magic ingredient which neutralizes the acid of the tomatoes so that the cream will not curdle.

2	**tablespoons butter**
⅓	**cup chopped onion**
1	**cup sliced carrots**
1	**(28 ounce) can diced tomatoes or 2 cups fresh tomatoes, peeled, seeded and puréed slightly in the processor**
1	**teaspoon dill**
¼	**teaspoon baking soda**
½	**cup chicken stock**
⅓	**cup rice (optional)**
1½	**cups milk**
½	**cup cream**
	Salt and cayenne

Sauté onions and carrots in butter for 10 minutes, stirring occasionally. Add tomatoes, dill, soda, stock and rice and simmer for 15 to 20 minutes. Add milk and cream and heat through. Taste for salt and cayenne. If you omit the rice, the soup will be much thinner.

Yield: 6 cups
Serves: 3-4

Green Chilies and Rice Soup

This recipe was originally a casserole. We added some chicken broth and milk and it became soup. Green chilies have a wonderful flavor. They are a little hot, so go lightly with the cayenne.

Sauté onions and garlic in butter over low heat for 10 minutes. Add stock, milk and rice and simmer for about 20 minutes. Add remaining ingredients and heat through over medium heat. Taste for seasoning.

Yield: 6 cups
Serves: 3-4

2	*tablespoons butter*
½	*cup chopped onion*
1	*garlic clove, minced*
2	*cups chicken stock*
1	*cup milk*
½	*cup raw rice*
2	*(4 ounce) cans diced green chilies*
2	*cups whipping cream*
½	*cup (2 ounces) shredded Monterey Jack cheese*
½	*cup (2 ounces) shredded process American cheese*
	Salt, cayenne, cumin to taste

Garnishes:

> *Diced tomatoes*
> *Avocado slices*
> *Tortilla chips*
> *Chopped cilantro*

Corn Chowder

⅓	cup diced salt pork
1	cup chopped onion
½	cup chopped green pepper
3	cups peeled and diced potatoes
1	cup chicken stock
2	cups milk
1½	cups whipping cream
2½	cups fresh or frozen cut corn
	Dash salt, pepper, nutmeg
	Crumbled bacon and chopped
	chives for garnish

In a large saucepan, fry pork until fat is rendered. Add onion and green pepper and sauté until tender. Add potatoes, chicken stock and milk and simmer for about 15 minutes. Add cream and corn and heat through. Finish the soup with seasonings to your taste.

Yield: 8 cups
Serves: 4-6

Lima Bean and Mushroom Chowder

Chowder has come a long way since the original version which was "a dish made of fresh clams or fish, pork, crackers, onions, etc. stewed together often in milk; now extended to cover combinations in which the fish is replaced by a vegetable." I have found that the one ingredient common to all "chowders" is potatoes. Potatoes and crackers are both used to give the chowder some body. Lima beans and mushrooms may sound like an unlikely twosome, but they produce a very flavorful combination.

Fry pork until crispy. Add onions and sauté for a few minutes. Add chicken stock, carrots, potatoes and seasonings and simmer for 15 minutes until tender. Add mushrooms and limas and cook for another 10 minutes. Finish with the whipping cream, salt, pepper and nutmeg to taste.

Yield: 6 cups
Serves: 3-4

⅓ **cup diced salt pork**
1 **cup chopped onion**
2 **cups chicken stock**
1 **cup sliced carrots**
1 **cup diced potatoes**
1 **pinch each thyme and rosemary**
1 **garlic clove, mashed**
1 **cup sliced mushrooms**
2 **cups frozen baby lima beans**
1½ **cups whipping cream**
Salt, pepper, nutmeg

Mushroom Chowder

2	*tablespoons butter*
½	*cup chopped onion*
½	*cup chopped celery*
1	*cup chicken stock*
1	*cup diced potatoes*
2	*cups milk*
6	*cups sliced mushrooms*
1	*cup whipping cream*
	Salt and pepper to taste
¼	*cup Sherry (optional)*

Sauté onion and celery in butter for 3 to 4 minutes. Add chicken stock and potatoes and simmer until tender. Add milk, cream and mushrooms and continue to cook for another 5 minutes. Correct seasoning and add sherry if you like. Let the chowder simmer for a little longer if you add the sherry.

Yield: 6 cups
Serves: 3-4

Brie Soup

Sauté onion, celery and mushroom in butter until tender. Add chicken stock and simmer for about 10 minutes. Trim off any skin on the Brie that is old. Brie is old when the skin begins to turn orange and smells like amonia. Add cheese to chicken stock and stir until it is melted. If you allow the mixture to boil at any time, the Brie will curdle, leaving a messy mass of cheese separated from the liquid. Remove from heat and cool. Process and return to saucepan. Add cream and heat through. Stir in parsley. Taste for seasoning. Garnish with chopped chives.

Yield: 4 cups
Serves: 2 to 3

½ cup chopped onion
½ cup chopped celery
½ cup chopped mushrooms
2 tablespoons butter
2 cups chicken stock
1 pound fresh Brie, cut into chunks
1 cup whipping cream
2 tablespoons chopped parsley
Chopped chives

BEAN TALK

As far as I'm concerned, beans are at their very best when used in soup. We have "souped" every kind of bean available in the southwest.

When I started testing bean soup recipes, it became apparent to me that it would be useful to include a few tips about dried beans. They should be soaked or their skins will be tough. If you are very organized, you'll wash the beans well, as some have a lot of dirt and rocks, and soak them in plenty of water overnight. If you haven't remembered to do this, you may wash them well, put them in a soup kettle with plenty of water, cover the pot and bring to a boil. Remove the kettle from the stove and just let the beans soak for an hour. Return the pot to the stove and proceed cooking. Actually, this quick-soak method is said to help retain the vitamins and produce fewer tough skins. Nutritionally, beans are high in protein, but they require the addition of rice to be a complete protein.

The following is a chart of all the beans with which I am familiar and their cooking times. Naturally, times will vary. Using a cover will speed cooking time, but keep a watch, because the water may boil away. I use a cover to bring the beans to a boil and then reduce the heat to medium low and let them simmer gently without the cover until they are tender. Also, don't stir them a lot or you will break their little skins. If you use the quick-soak method, the beans will cook in about half the time.

Beans	Cooking time, uncovered, medium heat
small white	2-3hours
black	2-3hours
pintos	1½hours
red	1½hours
blackeye	1½hours
navy	1½hours
great northern	1½hours
garbanzos	1½hours
limas	1hour
lentils	1hour
split peas	1hour

Since beans vary as to weight, it is impossible to give you any cups to pounds rule. Don't add salt to your beans until the end. Ham or salt pork will vary in salt content, and as the liquid cooks away, the flavor becomes stronger.

You may conjure up any kind of bean soup you like. Use pasta, basil, oregano, garlic and tomatoes with navy beans and you have Pasta and Fagioli. You can really spice up lentils with the addition of chorizo, garlic, comino and tomatoes. I hope that you enjoy experimenting with these recipes.

39

Arizona Mountain Soup

I believe that this is the first soup I ever made. It's a good, hearty one.
If it stands very long, however, it will turn to mush.

1½	cups dried pintos
1	ham hock or 4 ounces salt pork
8	slices thick bacon, diced
1½	cups chopped onion
2	garlic cloves, mashed
⅔	cup raw rice
1	(28 ounce) can tomatoes, diced
2	tablespoons chili powder
2	teaspoons comino
½	teaspoon paprika
	Salt and pepper

Pick over the pintos carefully as they usually contain a good portion of rocks. Wash them well. Soak in water overnight. Drain and put into a soup kettle with water to cover, along with ham hock or salt pork. Cover and bring to a boil; reduce heat and simmer for about an hour. Beans should be firm. Fry bacon in a skillet until crisp, add onion and garlic and fry for a couple of minutes, stirring. Add this to the beans. Add one cup water to the skillet and return it to the heat, stirring to remove all the good brown bits in the pan. This is an easy way to clean the pan too. Add this to pot along with 1 or 2 more cups of water and remaining ingredients, except salt and pepper. Simmer about 20 minutes more until the rice is cooked. Now season with salt and pepper to taste. Serve with jalapeno cornbread.

Yield: 6 cups
Serves: 3-4

Jota (Trieste-Style Bean, Potato, and Sauerkraut Soup)

I found this soup in an issue of GOURMET MAGAZINE. I have no idea of the meaning of Jota, but the recipe is definitely worth passing along. I included some sausage in addition to the ham hocks, but it is not necessary, especially if your ham hocks are very meaty.

Soak the beans overnight in 5 cups water or place in a saucepan, bring to a boil, cover and remove from heat for 1 hour. Drain beans and place in a heavy kettle with stock, ham hocks, onion, garlic and cornmeal and bring to a boil, stirring so that the cornmeal won't "lump up." Add bay leaf and sage and simmer for about an hour, until beans begin to be tender. Add sauerkraut, potatoes and sausage if desired and cook for another 20 minutes. Remove ham hocks, trim off ham and return to kettle with parsley and some freshly ground pepper. This soup should not require much salt as both the sauerkraut and ham hocks are quite salty.

1½	*cups red kidney beans, picked over and rinsed*
12	*cups chicken stock*
2	*ham hocks*
1½	*cups chopped onion*
2	*garlic cloves, minced*
3	*tablespoons yellow cornmeal*
1	*bay leaf*
1	*teaspoon sage*
1	*pound sauerkraut, rinsed well and squeezed dry*
4	*cups red potatoes, cut into 1 inch cubes*
2	*cups Kielbasa or any sausage you like, sliced (optional)*
½	*cup fresh parsley, minced*
	Salt and pepper

Yield: 16 cups
Serves: 10

Black Bean Soup

2½	*cups black beans, picked over and rinsed*
4	*ounces salt pork or a meaty ham hock*
2	*cups chopped onion*
½	*cup chopped parsley*
2	*large garlic cloves, mashed*
1	*teaspoon dried thyme*
1	*bay leaf*
1	*cup sliced carrots*
1	*cup sliced celery*
2	*teaspoons seasoning salt*
	Cayenne
½	*cup Sherry or Madiera (optional)*

Garnishes:

Grated hard boiled egg
Lemon slices
Sliced avocado
Sour cream
Chopped jalapenos
Monterey Jack cheese

Soak beans overnight in lots of water. Drain and put beans and pork or ham hock in a large soup kettle and add 3 quarts of water. Cover and bring to a boil. Then add onion, parsley, garlic, thyme and bay leaf. Simmer for about 30 minutes and add carrots and celery. Simmer for 2 to 3 more hours. Add season salt, cayenne and Sherry or Madiera at the last. You may purée the soup in a blender or food processor if you prefer a smooth soup. Chop the ham or pork and add it to the beans. This soup is better when reheated. It also freezes well.

Yield: 12 cups
Serves: 8

Blackeyed Pea Soup

I love blackeyed peas and I never get to have them except on New Years. Why not add a little stock and have soup?

Drain and put peas in a 3 quart saucepan with ham bone or salt pork and 5 cups water. Cover and bring to a boil. Reduce heat and simmer partially covered for 45 minutes. Add remaining ingredients and simmer over low heat for another 20 to 30 minutes. Remove ham from bone, chop it and return to pot. Correct seasoning with salt and pepper.

Yield: 6 cups
Serves: 3-4

1	*cup dried blackeyed peas, picked over and rinsed*
5	*cups water*
1	*meaty ham hock or 4 ounces salt pork, diced*
½	*cup chopped celery*
½	*cup chopped onion*
¼	*cup parsley*
¼	*cup red or green bell pepper*
1	*garlic clove, minced*
¼	*cup raw rice*
⅛	*teaspoon thyme*
	Salt and pepper

Garbanzo Bean Soup

Usually these beans are found along with pickled beets in salad bars.
They are ugly, but the soup is delicious.

1½	cups garbanzo beans (chick peas)
1	beef bone with some meat
1	ham bone with some meat
4	strips bacon, diced
1	cup onion, chopped
1	garlic clove, minced
1½	cups peeled and diced potatoes
	A pinch of saffron (optional)
	Salt and pepper
½	pound Chorizo or Kielbasa, sliced

Pick over the garbanzos carefully, wash them and put them in water. Add a tablespoon of salt and soak overnight. Drain the beans and put them in a soup pot with the bones and 2 quarts water. Bring to a boil and simmer for 45 minutes.

Fry bacon until crisp. Add onion and garlic and fry for 5 minutes. Add to the beans along with potatoes and saffron. Continue to cook for another 30 minutes. Garbanzos should not be overcooked; they become quite grainy. Remove the bones; take the meat from the bones and add it to the soup. Taste for salt and pepper. Fry sausage and serve it as a garnish.

Yield: 8-10 cups
Serves: 6

Lentil and Brown Rice Soup

In a large soup kettle, combine all ingredients except parsley, vinegar, salt and pepper. Bring to a boil and simmer the mixture for about 45 minutes to 1 hour. Stir in remaining ingredients and additional stock if necessary. Taste for seasoning.

Yield: 13-14 cups
Serves: 8

8	cups beef, chicken or lamb stock
1½	cups lentils, picked over and rinsed
1	cup brown rice
1	(28 ounce) can tomatoes, chopped, reserving the juice
2	cups sliced carrots
1½	cups chopped onion
1	cup chopped celery
3	garlic cloves, minced
½	teaspoon basil
½	teaspoon oregano
¼	teaspoon thyme
1	bay leaf
½	cup minced fresh parsley
1	tablespoon cider vinegar
	Salt and pepper to taste

Nine Bean Soup

Definitely a recipe to share with friends after you have made the nine pounds of soup mix.

One pound of each:

red
navy
pinto
black
blackeye
split pea
lentil
great northern
barley (a grain, not a bean)

2	cups nine bean soup mix
2	quarts water
1	ham hock with lots of meat
1½	cups chopped onion
1	garlic clove, minced
1	(28 ounce) can tomatoes, diced
1	(4 ounce) can chopped green chilies
	Salt and pepper

Wash beans well and soak overnight in water. Wait until you see the color of the water with all those beans! Put beans in a soup kettle with water, ham, onions and garlic. Cover and bring to a boil. Cook over medium heat for about 1½ hours. Add tomatoes and chilies and cook for another half hour. Correct seasoning with salt and pepper. Add a little chili powder if you like.

Yield: 14-16 cups
Serves: 8-10

Pasta and Fagioli Soup

Soak beans overnight in plenty of water. In a soup kettle, bring the beans, chicken stock and pork to a boil. Reduce heat and simmer for 30 to 45 minutes. Add garlic, herbs, onion, celery, carrots and tomatoes and continue simmering for 30 minutes until vegetables and beans are tender. Add pasta and sausage, cooking for 10 minutes more. Taste for salt and pepper. Pass the cheese as a garnish.

Yield: 12 cups
Serves: 8

2   cups navy beans, picked over and rinsed
2   quarts chicken stock
¼   pound salt pork, diced
1   garlic clove, mashed
1   teaspoon each oregano and basil
⅔   cup chopped onion
½   cup chopped celery
1   cup sliced carrots
1   (14½ ounce) can diced tomatoes
½   pound thick pasta, such as macaroni or rotini
1   pound Italian sausage, sliced
       Salt and pepper
       Freshly grated Parmesan cheese

Red Beans and Rice Soup

1	cup red kidney beans or pintos, picked over and rinsed
2	meaty ham hocks
1	cup chopped onion
1	cup sliced celery
1	cup diced green or red pepper
3	garlic cloves, minced
1	bay leaf
1	teaspoon cumin
½	teaspoon each thyme and basil
¾	cup raw rice
2	cups smoked pork sausage, chorizo or other spicy sausage Cayenne or Tabasco, salt

Soak beans overnight and drain. Add 8 cups water and ham hocks to the beans and bring to a boil. Reduce heat and simmer for an hour; beans should still be a bit crunchy. Now add vegetables, garlic, bay leaf, cumin, thyme, basil and rice. Continue simmering for another half hour, adding more water if necessary. Fry the sausage in a skillet until done, stirring to break it up. Remove with a slotted spoon and drain off most of the fat. With the skillet still over heat add ⅓ cup water, stirring to deglaze the pan. Add this flavorful goody to the soup kettle. Remove ham hocks and chop the meat. Return ham to soup and add salt and cayenne to taste.

Yield: 10 cups
Serves: 6

Spanish Sausage and Lentil Soup

If you want to get away from the same old humdrum lentil soup, try this one.

Heat olive oil in a 6 quart soup pot over medium heat. Add sausage and cook until most of the fat is rendered. Transfer sausage to platter. Drain off all but 2 tablespoons of fat from soup pot. Add ham, onion, green pepper and carrots, and cook for 15 minutes stirring occasionally. Add garlic and cook another 5 minutes. Add the bay leaf, thyme, cumin, stock, tomatoes and lentils and bring to a simmer. Lower heat, partially cover pot and simmer for 1 to 1½ hours, stirring occasionally. Add sausage to the pot at the end. Skim off any fat from the soup and correct seasoning with salt and pepper.

Yield: 12 cups
Serves: 8

1	*tablespoon olive oil*
1	*pound chorizo or other spicy garlic sausage*
½	*pound ham, diced*
1½	*cups chopped onion*
1	*cup chopped green pepper*
½	*cup sliced carrots*
2	*garlic cloves, minced*
1	*bay leaf*
¼	*teaspoon dried thyme*
½	*teaspoon ground cumin*
8-9	*cups rich chicken stock*
1	*(1 pound) can peeled tomatoes, diced*
1	*cup dried lentils, picked over and rinsed*
	Salt and pepper

Split Pea Soup

This old standby can be found on the back of the split pea package. I have simply made the ingredients a little more precise by calling for measurements.

1	**pound (2½ cups) split peas, picked over and rinsed**
1	**ham bone with lots of meat**
1½	**quarts water**
2	**tablespoons bacon drippings**
1½	**cups chopped onion**
1	**cup chopped celery with some leaves**
1	**cup sliced carrots**
	Salt and pepper
	Lemon juice

In a 3 or 4 quart saucepan, bring the peas, water and ham bone to a boil, reduce heat and simmer for 15 to 20 minutes. Sauté the vegetables in bacon drippings for 10 minutes. Add to the peas and continue simmering until the soup is the consistency you desire. Remove ham bone and dice the ham. Return ham to the soup and adjust the seasoning with salt, pepper and lemon juice.

Yield: 8 cups
Serves: 4-6

Stone Soup

You can depend on the French Apron to create something unusual.
The sweet potatoes give this soup its marvelous flavor. The beans give
the soup its name.

Fry pork until golden. Add sausage and fry until done. With a slotted spoon, remove meats from skillet and add to soup kettle. Drain off all but enough fat to sauté the onion. Add onion and cook until soft. Add to kettle. Use a little chicken stock to deglaze the skillet. Add this, beans and chicken stock to kettle and simmer for 30 to 45 minutes. Add remaining ingredients and continue simmering for 30 minutes, until vegetables are tender. You will have a mess if you overcook this soup. Taste for salt and pepper.

Yield: 14-16 cups
Serves: 8-10

¼	*pound salt pork, diced*
½	*pound spicy sausage, sliced or crumbled*
1	*cup chopped onion*
2	*cups red kidney beans, soaked overnight and drained*
2-3	*quarts chicken stock*
1	*pound zucchini, diced*
1	*pound sweet potatoes, peeled and diced*
1	*large garlic clove, mashed*
2	*cups peeled and diced potatoes*
	Salt and pepper
	Pimiento stuffed olives for garnish

51

U.S. Senate Bean Soup

This recipe came from THE GOURMET COOKBOOK, originally from the U.S. Senate Lunchroom which is where I sampled it many years ago.

2	*cups navy beans, picked over and rinsed*
1	*ham hock with lots of meat*
1	*cup cooked mashed potatoes*
1½	*cups chopped onions*
1½	*cups sliced celery, including leaves*
2	*garlic cloves, mashed*
¼	*cup chopped parsley*
	Salt and pepper to taste

Soak beans overnight in water. Drain and put the beans in a soup kettle with 3 quarts water and the ham bone. Bring water to a boil and simmer for about 2 hours or until beans are almost tender. Then add the vegetables, garlic and parsley and continue to simmer for 30 minutes, until vegetables are tender. Remove ham bone, dice meat and return it to the kettle. Taste for salt and pepper.

Yield: 8 cups
Serves: 4-6

Cream of Reuben Soup

This is the closest thing we have to sandwiches at The Buffet.

If you decide to buy a whole corned beef, prepare it according to the package instructions. Allow about three hours cooking time generally. Or you can buy a chunk of cooked corned beef and save all the bother. In a large saucepan, sauté onion and celery in butter until tender. Add stock, baking soda, and cornstarch and bring to a simmer, stirring. Add kraut, cream and corned beef and continue to simmer for about 15 to 20 minutes. Add cheese and cook until thoroughly blended. Correct the seasoning with salt and pepper if necessary. Be careful with the salt as many of the ingredients have a high salt content.

Yield: 6 cups
Serves: 3-4

1	*small corned beef or 2 cups (½ pound) cooked corned beef*
2	*tablespoons butter*
½	*cup sliced celery*
½	*cup chopped onion*
1	*cup chicken stock*
1	*cup beef stock*
½	*teaspoon baking soda*
1	*tablespoon cornstarch dissolved in*
2	*tablespoons water*
¾	*cup sauerkraut, drained and rinsed well*
2	*cups half and half or whipping cream or combination of both*
1	*cup (4 ounces) shredded process Swiss cheese*
	Salt and pepper

German Sausage Chowder

2	tablespoons butter
½	cup chopped onion
2	cups beef stock
2	cups peeled and diced potatoes
4	cups shredded cabbage
3	cups half and half
1	pound Kielbasa, Bratwurst, or Knockwurst, cut into ½ inch pieces
1	cup (4 ounces) shredded process Swiss cheese
	Season salt
	Dash pepper

Sauté onions in butter until tender. Add beef stock and potatoes and simmer for 15 minutes. Add cabbage and cream and simmer for 15 to 20 minutes or until cabbage is tender. Add remaining ingredients and simmer gently until heated through. Season to your taste. Serve with pumpernickle bread and beer.

Yield: 8 cups
Serves: 4-6

Sauerkraut Soup

8	cups beef stock
2	pounds sauerkraut
½	cup chopped onion
½	cup chopped celery
3	tablespoons butter or bacon drippings
¼	cup flour
½	teaspoon sweet Hungarian paprika
2	cups diced potatoes
½	pound Kielbasa, cut in ¼ inch slices
1	cup (4 ounces) grated Swiss cheese
	Pepper

Rinse kraut in a colander and drain it. Combine kraut and stock in a soup pot, bring to a boil and simmer for 30 minutes. In a large skillet, sauté onion and celery in butter or bacon drippings until soft, then add flour and paprika and cook, stirring for 3 to 5 minutes. Remove from heat and slowly stir in 2 cups of the stock. Add this to the remaining stock and kraut. Add potatoes and simmer for about 15 minutes. Then add Kielbasa and cook for another 5 to 10 minutes. Taste for seasoning. Garnish with Swiss cheese.

Yield: 10-12 cups
Serves: 6-8

Hungarian Paprika Soup

What a hit this soup was—we couldn't make enough. It came to me from a customer who had gotten it from the Fort Worth Club and we are most grateful to have it.

Brown the chili meat and onions in a large stockpot. (Only use oil if chili meat hasn't got enough fat.) Add the stock, paprika and tomato sauce and simmer for an hour, stirring occasionally. Add celery and carrots and cook until tender, about 20 to 30 minutes. Mix the butter and flour together and add enough of it to thicken your soup. Add noodles and simmer until they are done. At the last, correct the seasoning and stir in the sour cream. Do not let the soup boil or the cream will curdle. Or you may serve the sour cream as a garnish if you want to freeze part of the soup.

Yield: 12 cups
Serves: 8

2 pounds lean chili meat
1½ cups chopped onion
1-2 tablespoons oil (if necessary)
1½ to 2 quarts beef stock
3 tablespoons Hungarian paprika (you may use "hot" or you may use sweet and just add cayenne pepper to taste)
1½ cups tomato sauce
1 cup chopped celery
1 cup sliced carrots
2 tablespoons each butter and flour
2 cups noodles
1 cup sour cream
Salt, pepper, cayenne

Vegetable Beef Soup

2	tablespoons peanut or vegetable oil
1½	pounds lean stew meat
6	cups beef stock
1	cup chopped onion
1½	cups sliced carrots
1	cup sliced celery
1	cup cut corn
1½	cups peeled and diced potatoes
1	(14½ ounce) can diced tomatoes
1	large garlic clove, mashed
¼	teaspoon each basil, oregano and thyme
	Salt, pepper and paprika
	Splash of red wine (optional)

Pat the meat dry with paper towels; it will brown better. Sauté stew meat in oil, being careful to brown it on all sides. Add the beef stock and simmer until meat is tender, one to two hours, depending on the cut of meat. Add vegetables and seasonings and simmer for another 30 minutes until tender. Add the splash of wine at the last 5 minutes. Taste for seasoning. Feel free to substitute or add vegetables, mushrooms, green peas, green beans, zucchini or whatever you like.

Yield: 8 cups
Serves: 6

Brunswick Stew

This recipe originated in the Brunswick River area of Virginia and came to me from Mary Ellen DeLana, who also came from there. I believe that in the old days they used whatever sort of meat they captured that day: possum, squirrel, rabbit, etc. Most tidewater folk make the stew the day before serving, as the flavor improves when reheated.

In a soup kettle, sauté onions over medium heat until they begin to brown. Now dump remaining ingredients except salt and paprika into the kettle and simmer over low heat for a couple of hours. Add more chicken stock if necessary as the stew cooks. Correct seasoning at the end.

Yield: 14 cups
Serves: 7-8

2	tablespoons butter
1	cup chopped onion
1½	cups chicken stock
2	cups frozen baby lima beans
1½	cups cream style corn
2	cups fresh or frozen cut corn
2	(14½ ounce) cans tomato wedges
2	tablespoons Worcestershire sauce
3	tablespoons tomato paste
2	tablespoons lemon juice
2	cups diced, cooked ham
2	cups diced, raw chicken
	Lemon pepper, salt and paprika

Chicken Noodle Soup

2	tablespoons butter
¾	cup chopped onion
1½	quarts rich chicken stock
1	cup sliced carrots
¾	cup sliced celery
¼	cup chopped parsley
2	cups diced, cooked chicken
1	cup noodles
	Salt and pepper

Sauté onion in butter until soft. Add stock and vegetables and simmer until just tender. Then add chicken and noodles and simmer for about five minutes. Correct seasoning. The flavor of this soup is largely dependent on a good, flavorful stock.

Yield: 8 cups
Serves: 4-6

Cream of Chicken with Cheese Soup

I have found that process cheese is better for soups than natural cheese. Natural cheese when heated for very long will end up in a rubbery mass. You should also use process cheese in fondue.

4	tablespoons butter
¾	cup chopped onion
½	cup sliced carrots
½	cup sliced celery
1	quart chicken stock
1	cup whipping cream
1	pound grated American or Old English process cheese
3	cups chopped, cooked chicken
	Season salt and white pepper
	Chopped parsley

Sauté the vegetables in butter for about 10 minutes. Add chicken stock and cream and simmer until tender, about 15 minutes. Add cheese and chicken and simmer until hot. Season with salt and white pepper and garnish with parsley.

Yield: 8 cups
Serves: 4-6

Mulligatawny Soup

Mulligatawny comes from an Indian word, milakutanni, meaning pepper water. You may add as much curry as you like.

Sauté onion in butter until soft. Add carrots, green pepper, celery, rice and stock. Simmer for about 20 minutes. Add remaining ingredients and simmer until the apple is tender, about 10 to 15 minutes.

Yield: 8 cups
Serves: 4-6

4	*tablespoons butter*
1	*cup chopped onion*
1	*cup sliced carrots*
¾	*cup diced green pepper*
1	*cup sliced celery*
¼	*cup raw rice*
1	*quart chicken stock*
1	*medium, tart apple, cored and diced*
2	*cups chopped, cooked chicken*
¼	*cup minced parsley*
1	*(14½ ounce) can diced tomatoes*
2	*teaspoons curry powder*
½	*teaspoon garlic salt*
	Pepper

Bahamian Fish Chowder

I came across this recipe from Miss Madge Sawyer in LADY BROWN'S BAHAMIAN COOKBOOK, compiled by The Ladies of Nassau. The book is a delightful cross section of spicy native Bahamian cooking and such traditional English recipes as "rich tea biscuits" and "Christmas fruit cake."

¼	**pound salt pork or 6 pieces bacon, diced**
¾	**cup chopped onion**
3	**cups sliced potatoes**
1	**(14½ ounce) can tomato wedges or 1½ cups fresh tomatoes, peeled, seeded and diced**
3	**cups fish stock (Knorr's makes a good bouillon cube)**
½	**teaspoon thyme**
1	**pound firm white fish, cut into 1 inch cubes**
	Cayenne pepper and salt
	Lime wedges

Fry pork or bacon in a soup pot. When it begins to get crisp, add onion and cook, stirring occasionally, until onion is soft. Now add potatoes, tomatoes, fish stock and thyme and simmer for 15 to 20 minutes until potatoes are tender. Add fish cubes and simmer for another 5 minutes just to cook it. Taste for seasoning and serve with lime wedges. You may use a pound of whatever kind of seafood you like. The Bahamians would use grouper or conch.

Yield: 8 cups
Serves: 4-6

Clam Chowder

(If you use bacon, blanch in boiling water to remove some of the smokey taste which overwhelms the subtle taste of the clams. Pat dry.) In a saucepan, fry the bacon or pork until crisp. Add onion and sauté until tender. Stir in celery and cook for a couple of minutes. Add clam juice, half and half and potatoes and simmer for 20 minutes until potatoes are tender. Add clams and taste for seasoning.

If fresh clams are available, use about 1½ cups and 1½ cups of fish stock or bottled clam juice.

Yield: 8-10 cups
Serves: 6

2   strips of bacon or ½ cup salt pork, diced
½   cup chopped onion
¾   cup chopped celery
4   (6½ ounce) cans chopped clams, drained, reserving juice
3   cups diced potatoes
3   cups half and half
Salt and pepper

Monterey Fish Stew

¾   cup chopped onion
¼   cup chopped parsley
2   garlic cloves, mashed
2   tablespoons olive oil
1   cup chopped green pepper
1   cup sliced mushrooms
3-4 cups fish stock (Knorr's makes
     a good bouillon cube)
½   cup dry white wine
1   (14½ ounce) can tomato
     wedges or 1½ cups fresh
     tomatoes, peeled, seeded and
     diced
1½ cups diced potatoes
½   teaspoon thyme
¼   teaspoon each basil and
     marjoram
1   pound firm white fish such as
     cod, haddock or grouper, cut
     into 1 inch cubes
     Salt and pepper
     Juice of ½ lemon

In a soup kettle, sauté onion, parsley and garlic in olive oil over medium heat for 5 to 10 minutes. Stir in green peppers and mushrooms and cook for another 5 minutes. Add stock, wine, tomatoes, potatoes and seasonings and simmer for about 20 minutes, until potatoes are tender. Add fish just before you're ready to serve and cook for another 5 minutes. Correct seasoning with salt, pepper and lemon juice.

Yield: 8 cups
Serves: 4-6

Sausage and Clam Soup

Fry the sausage in a large saucepan. When it is done, drain off most of the fat, leaving just enough to cover the bottom of the pan. Add onions and mushrooms and cook for 10 minutes. Add garlic and cook, stirring for 5 minutes. Add remaining ingredients, except clams, and simmer for 20 minutes until vegetables are tender. Taste for seasoning and add parsley and clams.

Yield: 8 cups
Serves: 4-6

1½   pounds Italian sausage, sliced, or bulk sausage, crumbled
¾   cup chopped onion
1   cup sliced mushrooms
2   garlic cloves, minced
2   cups clam juice
½   cup dry vermouth or white wine
1   (14½ ounce) can diced tomatoes
¼   teaspoon each basil, thyme and oregano
¼   cup chopped fresh parsley
      Salt and dash cayenne or Tabasco
      Lemon juice
3   (6½ ounce) cans clams, drained, reserve broth

Sopa De Maiz (Mexican Corn Soup)

4	*tablespoons butter*
½	*cup chopped onion*
3½	*cups fresh or frozen cut corn*
1	*cup chicken stock*
1	*garlic clove, mashed*
1	*teaspoon cumin*
3	*tablespoons green chilies, chopped*
2	*cups half and half or milk*
1	*cup (4 ounces) shredded Monterey Jack cheese Salt and pepper to taste*
1	*(14½ ounce) can diced tomatoes, well drained, or*
1	*cup fresh tomatoes, peeled, seeded and chopped Chopped fresh parsley or cilantro*

Sauté onion in the butter until soft. Process half of the corn. Then add all the corn and the stock to the pan. Simmer until hot. Add the seasonings, chilies, and cream. Add cheese at the last, being careful not to boil the mixture or it will curdle. Taste for salt and pepper.

Divide the tomatoes between four bowls and ladle the hot soup over them. Garnish with parsley or cilantro.

Yield: 6 cups
Serves: 3-4

Poblano and Corn Soup

Cut pepper in half lengthwise. Cut out seeds and ribs, being careful to avoid touching the seeds as they are very hot. You may wear gloves if you prefer. Chop the pepper coarsely. Sauté pepper, onion and garlic in butter over low heat for 10 to 15 minutes, stirring occasionally. Add half and half, bouillon cube, cumin, cream style corn and 1 tablespoon parsley. Heat through. Taste for salt. Add a splash of Tabasco if you like it hot. Garnish with remaining parsley or cilantro.

Yield: 6 cups
Serves: 3-4

1	small poblano pepper
¾	cup chopped onion
2	garlic cloves, minced
3	tablespoons butter
1½	cups half and half
1	Knorr chicken bouillon cube
1½	teaspoons cumin
2	(17 ounce) cans cream style corn
2	tablespoons chopped Italian parsley or cilantro

Southwest Chicken Soup

In a soup kettle, sauté the onions and celery in the oil until soft. Add chicken stock, chicken pieces and brown rice. Bring mixture to a boil. Reduce heat, cover and simmer until chicken is tender, 20 to 30 minutes. Remove chicken and set aside to cool. Continue simmering for an additional 15 minutes. Remove chicken from bones and add to the stock along with remaining ingredients. Heat through and taste for seasoning.

Yield: 10-12 cups
Serves: 6-8

1	tablespoon olive oil
1	cup chopped onion
½	cup chopped celery
6	cups chicken stock
½	cup brown rice
1	(10 ounce) package frozen cut corn
4	chicken breasts
4	chicken thighs
1	teaspoon cumin
1	tablespoon chili powder
2	tablespoons picante sauce
1	(15½ ounce) can diced tomatoes
1	(4 ounce) can chopped green chilies

Black Bean Chili

This recipe appeared in BON APPETIT MAGAZINE *from Baron's Saloon in Denver. We have changed it a little, as the original recipe did not call for any chili powder.*

1	cup dried black beans
1	ham hock, or ¼ pound salt pork
1½	pounds stew meat, cut into ¾ inch cubes, patted dry
3	cups beef stock
½	cup chopped onions
¼	cup chopped green pepper
1	(28 ounce) can diced tomatoes
1	(4 ounce) can diced green chilies
3	tablespoons tomato paste
2	teaspoons cumin
1	tablespoon chili powder
2	garlic cloves, mashed
	Salt and pepper
1	cup (4 ounces) mixed grated Monterey and Cheddar cheese

Wash the beans well and soak overnight in water. Drain and pour into a soup pot. Add 3 cups water, ham hock or salt pork, cover, and bring to a boil. Reduce heat and simmer, covered, for an hour. Brown the stew meat in another large pot, then add beef stock and simmer this for an hour or until tender. Add beans and all remaining ingredients except salt, pepper and cheeses and simmer for another hour until the flavors meld. You may need to add more stock if the liquid cooks down. Remove ham hock or salt pork; chop meat and return to pot. Add salt and pepper to taste. Ladle into ovenproof containers, sprinkle with cheese, and place under a hot broiler to brown the cheese. This is a soup that gains flavor when reheated.

Yield: 8 cups
Serves: 4-6

Chili

There are as many different versions of chili as there are people who make it. This is a basic recipe. We prefer to let people season to their own tastes. If you like beans, add beans. If you like "Yankee" chili (ground meat and tomato sauce), cut down on the seasoning.

Brown the chili meat and onions together with a little oil if the meat is very lean. Add remaining ingredients and simmer slowly for an hour and a half. Serve the chili with grated cheese, tortilla chips and picante sauce.

Yield: 6 cups
Serves: 3-4

3½	*pounds lean chili meat*
2	*cups chopped onion*
1	*(14½ ounce) can diced tomatoes*
1	*(14½ ounce) can tomato sauce*
1	*cup beef broth*
2	*garlic cloves, mashed*
1	*teaspoon oregano*
¼	*cup chili powder*
2	*tablespoons ground cumin*
	Salt and cayenne

Guadalajara Pork Stew

Pat the meat dry with paper towels so that it will brown better and provide more flavor. Heat oil in a large soup kettle. Add meat and brown well. Add onion and garlic and sauté until golden. Stir in chili powder, oregano, cumin, beef stock and beans. Cover and simmer for about 1½ hours, until pork and beans are tender. (Soup may be prepared ahead to this point.)

Skim fat from broth. Heat broth to boiling; reduce heat, add chilies, carrots and corn and simmer for about 20 minutes. Season with salt and pepper if necessary.

Yield: 10-12 cups
Serves: 6-8

4	*pounds lean boneless pork shoulder, cut into 1" cubes*
1	*tablespoon oil*
1	*cup chopped onion*
2	*cloves garlic minced*
2	*tablespoons chili powder*
1	*teaspoon each oregano and cumin*
8	*cups beef stock*
1	*cup dried pinto beans, picked over and washed*
1	*(4 ounce) can chopped green chilies*
1	*cup sliced carrots*
1	*(10 ounce) package frozen cut corn*

Garnishes:

Cherry tomato halves	*Sour cream*
Sliced green onions	*Diced avocado*
Chopped fresh cilantro	*Lime wedges*
Salsa	

Tortilla Soup

1	cup chopped onion
2	garlic cloves, mashed
2	tablespoons oil
1	(4 ounce) can diced green chilies
1	(14½ ounce) can diced tomatoes
2	cups chicken stock
2	cups beef stock
1½	cups tomato juice
1	tablespoon cumin
1	tablespoon chili powder
1	tablespoon Worcestershire sauce
	Dash cayenne
½	cup (4 ounces) each shredded cheddar or Monterey Jack cheese
	Crisp tortilla chips
	Sour cream (optional)

In a large saucepan, sauté onion and garlic slowly in the oil for about 5 minutes. Add remaining ingredients, except chips and cheese, and simmer for ½ hour. You may add the chips to the soup or serve separately with the cheese. A dollop of sour cream is good too.

Yield: 7-8 cups
Serves: 4-6

Pot Luck Chili

"Pot Luck" is a wonderful term; it provides the license to use up almost anything you've got on hand. So feel free to add or delete anything except the meat, onions and chili.

Brown the stew meat in a soup kettle. Add beef stock and bring to a boil. Reduce heat slightly and cook at a hard simmer until tender, about an hour and a half. In the meantime, add 3 cups water to the pinto beans and bring to a boil. Remove from heat, cover, and let rest one hour. Sauté the sausage and drain off grease. When the meat is tender, add beans and remaining ingredients, except cheese and chips, and simmer for another 45 minutes. You may need to add more stock if the soup becomes too thick. Serve with chips or cornbread and grated cheese.

Yield: 16 cups
Serves: 10

3	*pounds lean beef stew meat or venison, patted dry*
2½	*quarts beef stock*
1	*cup dried pinto beans, picked over and washed*
1	*pound pork sausage*
2	*cups chopped onion*
1	*cup chopped celery*
1	*cup chopped green pepper*
3	*garlic cloves, minced*
1	*(28 ounce) can whole tomatoes, chopped, reserve juice*
1	*cup (8 ounces) diced green chilies*
1	*cup (8 ounces) diced pimientos*
1	*cup pitted ripe olives*
¼	*cup chili powder*
1	*tablespoon cumin*
1	*teaspoon oregano*
	Salt and cayenne to taste
	Grated Cheddar and Monterey Jack cheese
	Tortilla chips

69

Cold soups are not for everyone. For the devotee, here are a few of my ideas on the subject. Because our soup is being served as an entrée, I like to leave something to chew. I usually will not purée all the vegetables. The smooth consistency of a puréed soup is more suitable as a first course. Another consideration is that most people, when eating out, do not want to diet. I cannot deny that most of the cold soups served at the Kimbell are loaded with cream, sour cream, cream cheese or some combination of the three. Several customers have reported that they have successfully substituted yogurt for sour cream, or milk for cream. I have provided a basis for you to alter the recipes to suit your particular taste. A final word of caution: be sure to sample the soup for seasoning after it has been chilled. Chilling will reduce the flavor of any food. I have even chilled some disappointing red wines to make them palatable. Remember, too, a little fresh lemon juice will help heighten the flavor of almost any soup or sauce.

Avocado Soup

An easy way to remove avocados from the skin: cut the fruit lengthwise along the pit. Pull it apart and carefully push the seed out with the knife tip. Now use a serving spoon to scoop each half away from the skin. If you do this carefully the meat will come out quite smoothly. If not, you're going to chop these up anyway. Process all ingredients in batches and chill. Garnish with cilantro if you like it.

Yield: 4-5 cups
Serves: 3-4

3	large, ripe avocados (the dark, rough-skinned ones are best)
¼	cup chopped onion
1	cup chicken stock
½	cup sour cream
1¼	cups half and half
¼	cup lemon juice
1	garlic clove, mashed
	Salt and cayenne to taste

Cream of Artichoke Soup

2½   cups chicken stock
¼   cup chopped onion
½   cup sliced carrots
½   cup sliced mushrooms
¼   cup chopped parsley
¼   teaspoon thyme
½   teaspoon seasoning salt
2   (14 ounce) cans artichokes,
     drained
8   ounces cream cheese, softened
½   cup sour cream
2   cups whipping cream or
     half and half
     Dash of Tabasco

Simmer onion, carrots, mushrooms, parsley, thyme, seasoning salt for about 20 minutes. Set aside to cool. Process with artichokes, cream cheese and sour cream. Stir in whipping cream and taste for seasoning after well chilled.

Yield: 7-8 cups
Serves: 4-6

Broccoli Soup

In a large saucepan, sauté the onion until transparent. Add stock and seasonings and bring to a boil. If you use fresh broccoli, and you really should, peel off the tough outer layer of the stems and use them too. Add broccoli to saucepan and cook for a few minutes, until it is barely tender. It will continue to cook even after it has been removed from the stove, and it will turn yellow if you overcook it. Allow it to cool and process it. Season with salt, curry powder and lemon juice. The sour cream or yogurt may be added or served as a garnish with slices of lemon or lime.

Yield: 7 cups
Serves: 4

¾ *cup chopped onion*
1 *tablespoon butter*
2 *(10 ounce) packages frozen broccoli or 1½ pounds fresh broccoli, chopped*
3 *cups rich chicken stock*
⅛ *teaspoon salt*
1 *teaspoon curry powder*
1 *tablespoon lemon juice*
1½ *cups sour cream or yogurt*

75

Cream of Carrot Soup

¾   cup chopped onion
2¼   cups chicken stock
¾   cup milk
1   tablespoon dill
¼   teaspoon salt
     Dash sugar if carrots are not
     sweet
     Dash cayenne
6   cups sliced carrots
1½   cups whipping cream

Combine onion, stock, milk and seasonings in a large saucepan. Bring to a boil and boil for about 3 minutes. Add carrots; bring to a boil again. Reduce heat and simmer for about 10-15 minutes until carrots are just tender. Remove from heat and chill. Process until smooth and add whipping cream. Check seasoning.

Yield: 6 cups
Serves: 3-4

Cream of Cucumber Soup

Simmer potatoes, onion, stock, cucumbers, salt and pepper for 15 to 20 minutes, until vegetables are tender. Set aside to cool. In a food processor purée in batches the potato mixture and sour cream. Stir in half and half and taste for salt and pepper. Serve well chilled with a cucumber slice floating on top.

Yield: 8 cups
Serves: 4-6

3½   cups chicken stock
3   cups diced potatoes
¾   cup chopped onion
4   cups cucumbers, peeled, seeded
       and coarsely chopped
1   teaspoon salt
¼   teaspoon white pepper
½   cup sour cream
2   cups half and half

Cream of Green Chilies Soup

1½	cups chicken stock
¼	cup minced onion
1	small garlic clove, minced
8	ounces diced green chilies
2	(8-ounce) packages cream cheese, softened
1	cup sour cream
¼	teaspoon cumin
1	cup whipping cream or half and half
	Salt

Simmer chicken stock with minced onion for about 5 minutes. Set aside to cool. Purée all ingredients except whipping cream in a food processor until smooth. Whisk in cream and chill well. Taste for salt.

Yield: 6 cups
Serves: 3-4

Gazpacho

*The flavor of this soup is greatly heightened by fresh, ripe tomatoes.
In lieu of those, I prefer to use a good brand of canned ones. If you
like bell pepper, feel free to add some.*

You may either chop the vegetables
and mix all ingredients, or process
them or both, depending upon the
consistency you desire.

Yield: 7-8 cups
Serves: 4-6

4	*cups fresh tomatoes, peeled, seeded and chopped or 4 cups canned, diced tomatoes*
1	*cup cucumber, peeled, seeded and chopped*
½	*cup chopped onion*
1	*garlic clove*
1½	*cups tomato juice*
1	*tablespoon each red wine vinegar and lemon juice*
2	*tablespoons olive oil*
10	*pimiento stuffed olives*
2	*tablespoons Pace's medium picante sauce*
½	*teaspoon each basil and tarragon*
	Salt and Tabasco to taste
	Buttered croutons, avocado slices for garnish

Cream of Pimiento Soup

This soup would be wonderful made with fresh red bell peppers. They must be peeled and we don't have time to peel as many as we would require; but you can and here's how: roast the peppers under the broiler, turning frequently to blacken evenly. Remove from broiler and place in a brown bag for 10 to 15 minutes with the top closed. Remove and carefully peel off the skins. Or you can buy a little gadget which will peel the peppers. If you choose this method, you'll need to sauté the peppers in a little butter before processing.

½	cup chopped onion
2	tablespoons chopped parsley
1	cup chicken stock
8	ounces cream cheese, softened
½	cup sour cream
2	(4 ounce) jars pimientos or 2 red bell peppers
	Cayenne pepper
	Salt

Simmer onions and parsley in chicken stock for 15 minutes. Cool stock. Process in batches in a food processor. Hint: process cream cheese and sour cream together. Add a little stock and scrape down the sides. Process until smooth. Add a little more stock and process again, scraping down the sides. Then process pimientos or peppers and combine all. Chill well and taste for seasoning. Garnish with a sprig of fresh dill, parsley, basil or cilantro.

Yield: 3-4 cups
Serves: 2-3

Senegalese

Melt butter over medium heat. Add curry and cook for a minute. Stir in flour and cook until bubbly. Set the pan off the burner and stir in the stock with a wire whip. Return to heat and continue to cook until bubbly and thick. Chill well. Add the cream and whichever accompaniment you have chosen. Helen Corbitt loved to garnish this soup with a fresh edible flower. A nasturtium would be lovely.

Yield: 6 cups
Serves: 3-4

3	*tablespoons butter*
2	*teaspoons curry powder*
3	*tablespoons flour*
4	*cups strong chicken stock*
1½	*cups whipping cream*
1	*cup slivered white meat of chicken or 1 cup coarsely chopped shrimp or lobster or apples*
	Chopped chives for garnish

Vichyssoise

Yes, the classic recipe for this chilled potato soup does call for leeks. But, if you can't find them, the addition of more onion will produce a reasonable facsimile.

Sauté leeks and onion in butter until just golden, not brown. Add chicken stock, potatoes, parsley, salt and pepper. Simmer for about 30 minutes, until potatoes are tender. Allow mixture to cool and purée in batches in a blender or food processor. Stir in half and half and chill thoroughly. Taste for seasoning and garnish with chives.

Yield: 9-10 cups
Serves: 6-8

4	*leeks, white part only, washed well and thinly sliced*
¼	*cup chopped onion, or if lacking leeks, substitute*
1	*cup chopped onion*
1	*tablespoon butter*
1	*tablespoon chopped parsley*
4	*medium baking type potatoes, peeled and chopped*
1	*quart strong chicken stock (Knorr's cubes are not too bad in lieu of homemade stock)*
1	*teaspoon salt*
¼	*teaspoon white pepper*
1	*quart half and half*
	Fresh chopped chives for garnish

Spinach and Cucumber Soup

1	tablespoon butter
¾	cup chopped onion
2½	cups chicken stock
4	cups diced cucumbers
½	cup peeled, sliced potato
½	teaspoon salt
	Dash cayenne or Tabasco
1	tablespoon lemon juice
2	cups fresh spinach (tightly packed)
1	cup whipping cream

Sauté onions in butter in a large saucepan until tender. Add chicken stock, cucumbers, potatoes and seasonings and bring to a boil. Reduce heat and simmer for 15 to 20 minutes until potatoes are tender. Add spinach, remove from stove and cool. Process, add cream and chill. Check seasoning before serving.

Yield: 6-7 cups
Serves: 4

Tomato Cream Soup

Simmer onion and garlic in chicken stock for 5 minutes. Cool. Process lightly with remaining ingredients. Chill well. Taste for salt and cayenne.

Yield: 6 cups
Serves: 3-4

1	cup chicken stock
½	cup chopped onion
2	garlic cloves, mashed
2	(14½ ounce) cans Italian plum tomatoes or 3 cups fresh tomatoes, peeled, seeded and chopped
1	cup whipping cream
¼	cup sour cream
2	teaspoons dill or basil
1	tablespoon lemon juice
	Salt and cayenne to taste

Zucchini Soup

*Forget the diet with this selection. It just wouldn't be as good without
the cream cheese and sour cream. You could try yogurt if you're in a
mood to experiment.*

4	cups chicken stock
¾	cup chopped onion
5	cups zucchini, cut into chunks
1	heaping teaspoon dill
2	(8 ounce) packages cream cheese, softened
1	cup sour cream
¼	teaspoon salt
¼	teaspoon pepper

In a saucepan, bring the onion, stock and seasonings to a boil. Add zucchini, reduce heat, and simmer for 10 to 15 minutes. Do not let it become yellow and mushy! Let the mixture cool and process in batches with cream cheese and sour cream. Chill thoroughly. Taste for seasoning. Garnish with a sprig of fresh dill.

Yield: 10 cups
Serves: 6-8

Curried Zucchini Soup

This recipe came to me from Gretchen Hutton. I am always eternally grateful for the acquisition of a good cold soup that does not require cream. I suspect that broccoli or maybe green beans could be used in place of zucchini.

Sauté onion and garlic in oil until soft. Stir in curry powder. Add remaining ingredients and simmer until vegies are tender. Cool. Purée in a food processor. Chill well. Taste for seasonings. Serve with a dollop of yogurt, sour cream or crème fraîche.

Yield: 9-10 cups
Serves: 6-8

1	*tablespoon olive oil*
1	*cup chopped onion*
2	*garlic cloves, sliced*
2	*teaspoons curry powder*
6	*cups coarsely chopped zucchini*
3	*cups coarsely chopped russet potatoes*
1	*quart rich chicken stock*
	Salt and pepper to taste

Precolumbian, Huastec, A.D. 550-950,
Smiling Girl Holding a Basket, from Panuco Basin,
Northern Veracruz, ca. 600-800, clay

SALADS AND DRESSINGS

After experimenting with soups for three years, I welcomed the chance to turn my attention to another type of food. Originally, we served Buffet patrons a simple green salad with several choices of dressings. Sometimes there was salade niçoise, taco salad, or spinach salad as well, but that was all. Since salad bars have become the rage, it was natural for us to introduce one too, but not one featuring the ubiquitous pickled beets and garbanzo beans. It was my goal that even the determined dieter would be enticed by a delicious salad plate of fresh ingredients.

Salads are definitely as much fun as soups. There is no limit to the combinations you can create. Salad is not just iceburg lettuce and orange French dressing. It can introduce the meal, provide the meal or end the meal. The salad recipes presented here are intended to stimulate you to formulate your own creations based upon your own preferences.

Fresh ingredients are tremendously important in salads. Treat yourself: buy some really good extra virgin olive oil and balsamic vinegar to dress those fresh vegetables. You will taste the difference. Try walnut oil and hazelnut oil for a change. Yesterday's leftovers will never be recognized when presented in salad form.

Vinaigrette Dressing

You may use any kind and combinations of oils you like.

Shake together:

½	*teaspoon salt*
1	*teaspoon pepper*
1	*tablespoon Dijon-style mustard*
¼	*cup tarragon vinegar*
1	*tablespoon lemon juice*
1	*cup peanut oil*
¼	*cup olive oil*
2	*teaspoons fresh basil (¾ teaspoon dried)*
	Dash tarragon

TIP: Crush dried herbs in the palm of your hand or with a mortar and pestle to bring out the flavor.

Sweet and Sour Dressing

Mix the dry ingredients together with a little of the cider vinegar. Then stir in the remaining vinegar, onion, salad oil and ketchup and blend well.

Yield: 1¾ cups

½	*teaspoon garlic powder*
1	*tablespoon sugar*
1	*teaspoon dry mustard*
1	*teaspoon paprika*
¼	*teaspoon salt*
¼	*teaspoon pepper*
½	*cup cider vinegar*
2	*tablespoons minced onion*
¼	*cup salad oil*
¾	*cup ketchup or chili sauce*

Strawberry Vinaigrette

Here is a lovely light dressing for all sorts of fruits. Fill an avocado half with some canteloupe, blueberries, raspberries, strawberries, nuts, whatever you like; then drizzle some of this wonderful pink concoction over it.

1	cup strawberries, washed and hulled
¼	cup red wine vinegar
	Dash of sugar
1	cup olive oil

Process berries, vinegar and sugar. Slowly add oil to make an emulsion.

Yield: 2 cups

Blue Cheese Dressing

2	cups Hellman's or homemade mayonnaise
¾	cup buttermilk
1	tablespoon lemon juice
½	teaspoon garlic powder or 1 garlic clove, mashed
½	teaspoon lemon pepper
¼	cup crumbled blue cheese

Combine all ingredients except cheese which should be folded in last.

Yield: 3 cups

Avocado Dressing

Combine in a food processor until
well blended. Taste for seasoning.

Yield: 1¼ cups

*1   ripe, medium avocado, peeled
      and pitted*
*½   cup Slim Crème Fraîche
      (recipe below)*
1   garlic clove, mashed
2   tablespoons plain yogurt
1   tablespoon red wine vinegar
*½   teaspoon salt
      Dash Tabasco or cayenne*

Slim Crème Fraîche

Combine in a glass jar and shake for
1 minute. Let stand in a warm place
until thick (this will take from 4 to
24 hours depending upon the
weather). *Crème fraîche* may be
stored in refrigerator up to 3 weeks.

Yield: 2 cups

2   cups half and half
1½   tablespoons buttermilk

Sour Cream and Dill Dressing

1 cup Hellman's or homemade
  mayonnaise
1¼ cup sour cream
¾ cup buttermilk
¾ teaspoon dill
1 tablespoon Dijon-style or
  Creole mustard
  Freshly grated pepper

Mix all ingredients well.

Yield: 3 cups

Crème Fraîche

2 cups whipping cream
2 tablespoons buttermilk

Combine cream and buttermilk in a jar and shake for 1 minute. Allow to stand at room temperature for 12 hours. *Crème fraîche* will keep for 2 to 3 weeks in the fridge. It is great on berries (sweeten with a little brown sugar or honey if you like). It is wonderful for use in sauces; it doesn't curdle as does sour cream.

Yield: 2 cups

94

Macaroni Salad

Cook the macaroni in boiling water to which you have added a few drops of oil to keep the water from boiling over. Stir occasionally at the beginning or pasta will all stick to the bottom. Keep the water at a gentle boil for about 5 minutes. For salads you want your pasta to be "al dente," otherwise you end up with a mushy mess when you try to combine all the ingredients. Drain macaroni and rinse with cold water, tossing lightly. The rest is a snap: lightly toss all ingredients and chill.

Yield: 5 cups
Serves: 6-8

1½	*cups uncooked macaroni*
½	*cup Hellman's or homemade mayonnaise*
⅓	*cup vinaigrette dressing*
⅓	*cup chopped pimientos*
⅔	*cup sliced ripe olives*
¼	*cup minced onion*
¼	*cup chopped green pepper*
1½	*cups grated Cheddar or Swiss cheese*
1	*cup coarsely ground ham or crumbled cooked bacon*
	Salt and pepper to taste

Pasta Salad

2½	cups medium noodles, such as fettucini
½	cup vinaigrette dressing
1½	cups blanched broccoli florets or 1 cup packed raw spinach
1	(2 ounce) jar diced pimiento
12	pitted ripe olives, sliced lengthwise
½	cup mushrooms, sliced

We use a mixture of half spinach noodles and half egg noodles. Really you may use most any sort of pasta you have on hand; of course, fresh pasta is ideal. Put pasta in three quarts of boiling salted water, to which ½ teaspoon of salad or olive oil has been added to prevent sticking or boiling over. Cook 4 or 5 minutes, stirring occasionally. Drain the pasta and refresh with cold water. Toss pasta in a large bowl with two or three tablespoons of the dressing just to coat it. Let the pasta cool. Toss with the vegetables, add more dressing, salt, and pepper if necessary.

This is a very versatile salad. Instead of the broccoli or spinach you could use sliced zucchini, yellow squash, fresh green beans, asparagus, English peas, or artichoke hearts. Tuna, chicken, salami, Greek olives, chopped red, yellow or green bell pepper are some other ideas. Use mayonnaise rather than vinaigrette if you like. Freshly grated Parmesan cheese is a nice topping.

Yield: 5-6 cups
Serves: 6-8

French Apron Sicilian Pasta Salad

Cook pasta in water with a little salt and olive oil according to instructions. Drain in a colander and toss with enough olive oil to *lightly* coat it. Cook shrimp in boiling, salted water just until they turn pink. Drain and set aside to cool.

12	*ounces fettucine-style pasta (homemade preferrably)*
¾	*pound raw shrimp, shelled and deveined*
⅓	*cup pistachios, peeled and coarsely chopped*
1	*recipe Red Pepper Sauce (below)*

Red Pepper Sauce

Broil the peppers on rack in oven, 6 inches from heat, turning until they are black all over. Place then in a paper bag until cool, about 20 to 30 minutes. Peel off skins and remove stem and seeds, catching the juice in a bowl. Purée in a food processor with yogurt, salt and cayenne until smooth.

Arrange pasta on a salad plate and top with the sauce. Garnish with shrimp and pistachios.

Yield: 4-6 servings

3	*red bell peppers*
¼	*cup yogurt*
	Dash salt and cayenne

French Apron Rice Salad

1	cup uncooked rice
½	cup (2 ounces) salami, diced
½	cup (2 ounces) Fontina cheese, diced
¼	cup (1 ounce) pepperoni, diced
¾	cup (6 ounces) pickled brussel sprouts or any pickled vegetable
¾	cup (6 ounces) marinated artichokes, coarsley chopped
1	tablespoon capers
3	tablespoons sliced pitted ripe olives
¾	cup diced zucchini
⅓	cup olive oil
	Juice of one lemon
1	teaspoon basil
¼	teaspoon salt
	Pepper

Bring two quarts of salted water to a boil. Add rice and continue to boil, uncovered, for 13 minutes. Drain and refresh with cold water. Add lemon juice and olive oil. Toss in the chopped ingredients. Add seasonings and serve in a lettuce-lined bowl.

Yield: 5-6 cups
Serves: 10-12

Rice Salad

Toss hot rice with reserved marinade. Set aside to cool. Toss lightly with remaining ingredients. Add olive oil if necessary to moisten. Serve at room temperature.

I have used halved cherry tomatoes, sliced red bell pepper or sliced pimiento when good fresh tomatoes are not available. One cup of washed and stemmed fresh spinach is good in place of or in addition to the artichokes. For large portions I use our vinaigrette dressing rather than the artichoke marinade and the olive oil. Be creative. You could also use some diced cooked chicken, tuna, even Kielbasa. French cut green beans, water chestnuts, celery, etc. would be good.

Yield: 6 cups
Serves: 6-8

3 cups hot cooked white rice or Uncle Ben's wild and white rice or brown rice

1 cup marinated artichoke hearts, cut into chunks— reserve the marinade

½ pound sliced fresh mushrooms

1 cup fresh tomatoes, peeled, seeded and chopped

½ cup sliced black olives

½ small purple onion, sliced

½ cup toasted sliced almonds or other nuts

Olive oil to moisten

Rice Salad

3	cups cooked rice
¼	cup water chestnuts
¼	cup mushrooms
2	tablespoons minced parsley
½	cup artichoke hearts
2	tablespoons minced onion
2	tablespoons diced pimientos
1	teaspoon curry powder
½	cup mayonnaise
¼	cup sour cream
	Salt and pepper to taste

Gently combine all ingredients. Refrigerate. Serve on a bed of red leaf or Bibb lettuce.

Yield: 4-5 cups
Serves: 6

Cracked Wheat Salad

Cracked wheat, also known as bulgur, is used in tabbouleh, a tasteful salad originating in the Middle East. We use tabbouleh as a base for a lot of vegetable salads. The addition of a legume provides a source of complete protein.

2	cups cracked wheat
1½	cups water
½	cup lemon juice
½	cup olive oil
1	heaping teaspoon lemon pepper
½	cup chopped parsley or mint

Soak the wheat in the water in a large bowl until all the water is absorbed. Allow about an hour. Then toss with the remaining ingredients.

We add to the wheat any of the following vegetables and legumes:

Ripe olives	Brussel sprouts
Tomatoes	Lentils
Cucumbers	Garbanzo beans
Zucchini	Black beans
Green beans	Blackeye peas
Green onions	And so on and so on

If you are adding a lot of vegetables, you may need to add more lemon juice and olive oil. The wheat should be allowed to absorb the flavors for 2 or 3 hours after being dressed.

Yield will vary with addition of ingredients.

White Bean and Tuna Salad

Actually, you may substitute any sort of bean that turns you on. This is a good base for bean salad. You may substitute black beans, lentils, or kidneys. We use red peppers in place of celery because of the bright red color, but they are not always available. Sometimes we use ham rather than tuna; or no meat at all.

In a large bowl, whisk together vinegar, mustard, salt and pepper. Add oil in a thin stream, whisking to make an emulsion. Add beans, onion, celery, 2 tablespoons parsley, dill and tuna and toss lightly so as not to damage the beans. Garnish with remaining parsley.

Yield: 4 cups
Serves: 4-6

2	*tablespoons red wine vinegar*
1	*teaspoon Dijon-style mustard*
	Salt and pepper to taste
1/3	*cup vegetable or olive oil*
3	*cups cooked and drained white beans*
1/2	*cup sliced green onion, including some green tops*
1/2	*cup sliced celery or diced red pepper*
1/4	*cup chopped parsley*
2	*tablespoons minced fresh dill or a scant tablespoon dried dill or basil*
1	*(7 ounce) can tuna, drained and flaked*

Kraut Salad

This sweet and tart flavor adds a different touch to a picnic. It's really nice with hamburgers or fried chicken.

1	*quart sauerkraut, washed and drained*
1½	*cups diced green pepper*
1½	*cups sliced green onions*
½	*cup sliced celery*
1½	*cups cider vinegar*
1½	*cups sugar*

Combine kraut and vegetables in a large bowl. Heat vinegar and sugar to boiling. Cool and pour over vegetables. Store in a container in the refrigerator for 48 hours prior to serving.

Yield: 6 cups
Serves: 12-14

Pea Salad

6	*cups frozen, cooked peas*
¼	*cup chopped pimientos*
1	*cup chopped ham*
1	*cup grated Swiss or American cheese*
2	*tablespoons minced onion*
½	*cup sour cream*
¼	*cup mayonnaise*
1	*teaspoon Dijon-style mustard*
½	*teaspoon dried dill*
	Salt and pepper to taste

This is difficult, so pay close attention to these instructions: Combine all and mix gently.

Yield: 8 cups
Serves: 10-12

Snow Pea Salad

Cut snow peas in half on the diagonal. Blanch in 2 quarts of boiling water for 1 minute. Drain and refresh under cold water. Slice mushrooms. Slice pepper in ¼ inch slices. Brown sesame seeds in small skillet over moderate heat for a minute or two. Set aside to cool. Whisk together oil, vinegar, lemon juice, sugar, salt and pepper until thick. Pour over vegetables and toss gently. Sprinkle with sesame seeds.

Yield: 4-6 servings

½ *pound fresh snow peas, strings removed*
½ *pound mushrooms, stems removed*
1 *large red bell pepper, cored and seeded (green may be used if red is not available)*
2 *tablespoons sesame seeds*
1 *garlic clove, mashed*
⅓ *cup vegetable or peanut oil*
2 *tablespoons white wine vinegar*
1 *tablespoon lemon juice*
½ *teaspoon sugar*
Salt and pepper

Fresh Tomato and Mozzarella Salad

Don't even bother with this salad unless you can get wonderful vine-ripe tomatoes and fresh Mozzarella. You can't make the pesto sauce without fresh basil.

4	**large ripe tomatoes**
8	**ounces fresh Mozzarella, Italian Fontina, or Bel Paese cheese**
½	**cup fresh basil pesto, room temperature (recipe page 105)**
¼ to ½	**cup virgin olive oil**
	Freshly ground pepper

Slice tomatoes into 4 or 5 slices. Slice cheese into thin slices to equal tomato slices. Arrange slices on salad plates in overlapping slices with cheese on top of tomato. Spread a thin layer of pesto over cheese. Pass olive oil, salt and pepper. The salad is good with only olive oil if you don't want to do the pesto.

Serves: 4

Fresh Basil Pesto

Make large quantities while basil is at its prime and freeze to be enjoyed year round. Pesto is also great served warm over homemade pasta.

Place basil leaves in food processor with the metal blade. With machine running, drop in garlic cloves. Scrape down sides of the bowl. Add pine nuts and cheese and process until smooth. With machine running, pour olive oil through feed tube in a slow, steady stream and mix until smooth and creamy. If pesto is too thick or pasty, gradually add up to ¼ cup hot water through the feed tube with machine running. Transfer pesto to a jar. Cover surface with a film of olive oil. Seal with a tight-fitting lid. Refrigerate up to 3 months or freeze. Stir in oil before using.

Yield: 1½ cups

2	*cups packed fresh basil leaves*
2	*large garlic cloves*
½	*cup pine nuts*
¾	*cup freshly grated Parmesan cheese*
⅔	*cup olive oil*

Marinated Vegetables

In addition to or in place of any of the following vegetables, you might try: zucchini, asparagus, snow peas, broccoli, cauliflower, celery, water chestnuts, to name a few. Blanch the vegetables or leave them raw.

2   **pints cherry tomatoes, cut in half**

1   **small red onion, thinly sliced**

1   **can pitted black olives, drained**

2   **pints mushrooms, sliced**

2   **(8½ ounce) cans artichoke hearts, drained**

1   **cup (4 ounces) shredded Mozzarella cheese**

Marinate all ingredients overnight in vinaigrette dressing.

Yield: 8 cups
Serves: 12-16

Mushroom Cheese Salad

Lightly toss the ingredients and serve
chilled or at room temperature on a
bed of red leaf lettuce.

Yield: 8 cups
Serves: 12-16

1   (6 ounce) can pitted ripe olives
1   pound (4½ cups) mushrooms,
    sliced
2   bunches green onions, sliced
¼   cup chopped parsley
1   pound Swiss or Mozzarella
    cheese, grated or cut into
    julienne
2   teaspoons Cavender's Greek
    Seasoning
2   tablespoons olive oil
¼   cup vinegar

Swiss Cheese Salad

1	*pound grated Swiss cheese*
1½	*cups sausage, salami or ham, diced*
¼	*cup chopped parsley*
¼	*cup minced onion*
½	*cup sliced ripe olives*
¼	*cup vinaigrette*
½	*cup mayonnaise*
⅓	*cup sour cream*

Combine all ingredients and serve chilled.

Yield: 5 cups
Serves: 6-8

Egg Salad

Peel eggs and quarter them. Place in a bowl with the onion. Mix together remaining ingredients and toss gently with eggs. If you like a zestier version, add more onion and more mustard. Sometimes I add a little sweet pickle relish or some chopped dill pickle. I love egg salad served on black bread or pumpernickle.

Yield: 3 cups
Serves: 4-6

8	*hard-cooked eggs*
2	*tablespoons chopped purple onion*
½	*teaspoon dill*
½	*cup Hellman's or homemade mayonnaise*
¼	*cup sour cream*
2	*teaspoons Dijon-style mustard*
	Salt and grated pepper

TIP: There are a few tips for producing the perfect boiled egg. Of course, your eggs should be fresh. Let them get to room temperature and then place in saucepan and cover with lightly salted water. Bring to a boil over high heat, stirring gently to set the yolk in the middle of the egg. Boil for 12 to 15 minutes. Remove from heat and drain off hot water. Immediately immerse in ice water. Peel the eggs as soon as they are cool. They may be stored covered in the fridge for 2 or 3 days. If you need to keep them longer, leave in gently cracked shells. I've kept them up to a week.

Chicken Salad

4	*cups diced, cooked chicken*
2	*tablespoons minced onion*
1/3	*cup diced celery*
1/2	*cup sour cream*
1/2	*cup mayonnaise*
	Salt and pepper

Optional Ingredients:

1/2	*cup diced avocado*
1/2	*cup diced pineapple*
1/2	*cup halved grapes*
1/2	*cup toasted slivered almonds*
	or
1/2	*cup pecan pieces*

Gently toss the ingredients. Serve well chilled on a bed of Boston lettuce. Add any combination of the optional ingredients.

Yield: 5-6 cups
Serves: 4

Sesame Chicken Salad

Lightly toss all ingredients with dressing. Add salt and pepper to your taste. Blanched snow peas would be a nice addition or replacement for the pepper.

Yield: 8-9 cups
Serves: 6-8

½	*cup sliced green onion*
½	*cup minced green or red pepper*
2	*cups diced chicken*
2	*cups diced ham*
1	*cup diced Swiss cheese*
½	*cup toasted sesame seeds*
½	*cup toasted pecans, almonds, walnuts, or hazelnuts*
1	*cup cooked pasta*

Dressing:

2	*tablespoons Dijon-style mustard*
½	*teaspoon dry mustard*
¾	*cup cider vinegar*
¼	*cup honey*
½	*teaspoon garlic powder*
1	*cup peanut oil*
2	*tablespoons sesame oil (optional)*

French Apron Pâté Salad

I love this salad. It is not one that would benefit from substitutions. Use a good pâté and try to find the haricots verts.

¼	*cup walnut oil*
¼	*cup olive oil*
½	*cup chopped walnuts*
¼	*cup chopped green onions*
¼	*cup red wine vinegar*
1	*teaspoon dry mustard*
1½	*pound small green beans (haricots verts, available at specialty food stores)*
2	*medium red delicious apples*
	Lemon Juice
	Salt and freshly ground pepper
	Bibb lettuce
12	*(¾ pound) pâté, chilled and cut into ¼ inch dice*

Combine oils, ¼ cup of walnuts, onion, vinegar, mustard and salt to taste in processor until smooth. Cook beans in boiling, salted water for a minute or two. Drain in a colander and refresh with cold water. Set aside to cool, then toss with dressing and chill overnight.

One hour before serving, core apples and cut into julienne. Sprinkle with lemon juice and add to green beans with remaining ¼ cup walnuts. Add salt and pepper to taste. Just before serving, arrange lettuce leaves on salad plates. Spoon green beans onto lettuce and top with diced pâté. Serve at room temperature.

Yield: 10 servings

Scallop Salad

Wash scallops in a colander. If you are using the larger sea scallops, slice them into 2 or 3 sections. Steam them for about 5 minutes. Don't overcook or they will become tough. Drain and pat dry. Pull the strings from the snow peas and wash them. Blanch in boiling water for 1 minute. Drain and refresh with cold water. Pat dry. Toss scallops, mushrooms and snow peas lightly and chill. Arrange lettuce on 4 salad plates. Spoon scallop mixture onto lettuce and top with mayonnaise. Sometimes I substitute an avocado for the snow peas.

Yield: 4 servings

Note: This salad works well on a buffet table also. Increase the recipe 10 times and toss with vinaigrette dressing only. Serve in a lettuce lined bowl.

Yield: 30-35 servings

1	*pound bay scallops or sea scallops*
¼	*pound mushrooms, sliced*
¼	*pound snow peas*
¼	*cup mayonnaise, thinned with a little vinaigrette dressing*
	Boston lettuce

Smoked Turkey Salad

Ham, turkey or Kielbasa would all be good in place of the smoked turkey.

4	**cups (1½ pounds) diced smoked turkey**
1	**cup red seedless grapes, sliced in half**
1	**cup grated Swiss or Jarlsburg cheese**
¼	**cup sliced celery**
¼	**cup sliced almonds, toasted or walnuts or pecans**
¾	**cup mayonnaise**
¾	**cup sour cream**
	Salt and pepper

Gently combine all ingredients and add salt and pepper to your taste. Serve chilled on a bed of Bibb lettuce or radiccio.

Yield: 6 cups
Serves: 6-8

Smoked Turkey and Potato Salad

I love potato skins so I leave them on; but if you don't, take them off. Bring potatoes to a boil in salted water. Reduce heat and simmer for about 10 minutes. Watch it or you'll have mashed potatoes. Drain potatoes and refresh with cold water. Blanch green beans in boiling water for 3 minutes. Drain and refresh with cold water. Mix seasonings with mayonnaise and sour cream and toss all ingredients lightly. Or toss lightly with vinaigrette dressing.

Yield: 6-7 cups
Serves: 8-10

4	*cups diced new potatoes*
¼	*cup minced onion*
2	*cups diced smoked turkey*
¼	*cup chopped parsley*
1	*cup fresh cut green beans (optional)*
1	*teaspoon dill (optional)*
	Salt and pepper
½	*cup mayonnaise with ¾ cup sour cream or*
¾	*cup vinaigrette dressing, alone*

Vinaigrette Dressing

Mix together the vinegar, salt, mustard, and pepper. Slowly add oil, stirring to make an emulsion.

½	*cup oil*
¼	*cup vinegar or lemon juice or both*
¼	*teaspoon salt*
1	*teaspoon Dijon-style mustard*
	Freshly grated pepper

DESSERTS

Baking is not one of the things I do best, largely because it requires some degree of organization. I find that if I begin by reviewing the entire recipe, then assembling all the ingredients, I am fairly successful. Unless otherwise specified you should preheat the oven, place the rack in the middle of the oven and prepare your pans before mixing begins. We use a non-stick pan coating on our 9 × 13 inch pans, but we frost and serve the cakes directly from the pan. We find that we have to grease and flour the Bundt pans to prevent the cakes from sticking. Generally speaking, if you want to be assured of presenting a pretty cake, you had better do the "grease and flour" routine. I have found that shortcuts do not usually produce satisfactory results.

When you divide a recipe in half or double or triple it, calculate all the measurements before you begin. Write it all down and then check it again.

I love the unusual flavor of Mexican vanilla. If you can't go to Mexico to get it, it is available at some Mexican restaurants. Try it in whipped cream, ice cream and chocolate desserts.

When you are measuring flour, be sure to sift if sifting is required. Then measure the amount, don't shake the cup to level the measurement, smooth it with a knife.

One stick of butter equals 8 tablespoons or ½ cup. There are four sticks to a pound, or 2 cups.

Melt chocolate very slowly or it will "harden" into an unworkable mass.

Finally, I love to experiment, but during the baking process, there are a number of chemical actions occurring. I do not understand these processes well enough yet to try to tamper with them. So, while you may change the flavorings to suit your own tastes, you should not change the basic proportions of flour, sugar, baking powder and liquid.

DESSERTS

Tips for beating egg whites:

1. "Squeaky clean" utensils, free of grease.
2. Fresh eggs.
3. Separate eggs while they are cold. The yolks will not break as readily as when they have reached room temperature.
4. Allow whites to reach room temperature before beating.
5. Commence the beating process on low speed and continue until the whites become frothy.
6. Move to medium speed and beat until whites are thick. Add cream of tartar at this point.
7. Finish beating on high speed just until whites are stiff and shiny.

Underbeaten eggs will not be fluffy and voluminous. Overbeaten eggs will lose all the volume you have beaten in and will form clumps which will be difficult to blend with other ingredients.

More egg tips:

1. Lightly beaten means to use a fork or whisk to beat the eggs just until they are combined.
2. Well-beaten means to use a mixer to beat the eggs until they are pale and fluffy.
3. When adding sugar to eggs, yolks or whites, add it slowly for a lighter product.
4. When combining egg whites with another mixture, begin by incorporating about one third of the whites into the heavier mixture to lighten it. Then gently fold in the remaining whites.
5. When combining eggs with a hot mixture, stir a little of the hot mixture into the eggs, then a little more until the eggs are hot. Now add egg mixture to remaining hot mixture. This procedure prevents "scrambling" the eggs.
6. We use large eggs in all of these recipes.

Anna's Chocolate Cake

When I opened The Buffet, I was fortunate to inherit "the veteran baker," Anna Spencer, because I'm not really a baker. She was kind enough to share several cake recipes with me. I like this recipe so well that I asked Anna to bake it for my wedding cake!

Preheat oven to 350°. Butter and flour a 9 × 13 inch pan. Heat butter, water and cocoa over low heat until butter is melted. Let cool. Add to flour and sugar and mix well. Add remaining ingredients, mixing after each addition. Pour into prepared pan and bake for 30 minutes.

2	*sticks butter or margarine*
1	*cup water*
¼	*cup cocoa*
2	*cups flour*
2	*cups sugar*
2	*eggs*
½	*cup buttermilk*
1	*teaspoon soda*
1	*teaspoon vanilla*

Chocolate Frosting:

1	*stick butter*
¼	*cup cocoa*
¼	*cup buttermilk*
2	*cups powdered sugar*

Heat butter, cocoa, and buttermilk over low heat until butter is melted. (It looks like a mess!) Add to the powdered sugar and beat well. While cake is still warm, spread with frosting.

Yield: 16 servings

German Chocolate Cake

Yes, we do occasionally use cake mixes at The Buffet—why make life difficult?

1	**box yellow cake mix**
1	**small package Jello instant vanilla pudding**
4	**ounces German chocolate**
4	**eggs**
¼	**cup Crisco oil**
1¼	**cups buttermilk**

Preheat oven to 325°. Grease and flour a 9×13 inch pan. Melt chocolate over hot water or over very low heat. Cool. Combine all ingredients, mixing well. Pour into prepared pan and bake for 30 minutes. Cool.

Topping:

1	**cup evaporated milk or whipping cream**
1	**cup sugar**
3	**egg yolks, slightly beaten**
1	**stick butter**
1	**teaspoon vanilla**
1	**cup chopped pecans**
½	**cup coconut**

Combine milk, sugar, egg yolks, and butter. Cook over medium heat, stirring and stirring and stirring, until the mixture thickens—about 12 minutes. Remove from heat, add pecans and coconut and cool—over an ice bath if you're in a hurry—stirring occasionally. Spread on top of cake.

Yield: 16 servings

Oatmeal Cake

Although oatmeal does not sound like a very good base for a cake, try this; it's one of our most popular cakes.

Preheat oven to 350°. Grease a 9 × 13 inch pan. Add boiling water to oats and set aside. Cream the sugars and butter and add eggs and vanilla, mixing well. Next add cooled oats. Mix in dry ingredients. Pour into prepared pan.

1	cup oats
1¼	cups boiling water
1	cup brown sugar, lightly packed
1	cup white sugar
1	stick butter or margarine
2	eggs, beaten
1½	cups flour
1	teaspoon vanilla
2	teaspoons soda
2	teaspoons cinnamon
½	teaspoon nutmeg

Sprinkle coconut and pecans on unbaked cake. Mix together topping ingredients and pour over cake. Bake for 40 minutes.

Yield: 16 servings

Topping:

1	cup coconut
1	cup chopped pecans
3	tablespoons milk
3	tablespoons melted butter or margarine
1	teaspoon vanilla
2	egg yolks
1	cup brown sugar

German Apple Cake

2	eggs
1	cup oil
2	cups sugar
1	teaspoon vanilla
1	teaspoon cinnamon
½	teaspoon nutmeg
¼	teaspoon cloves
1	teaspoon baking soda
2	cups flour
½	teaspoon salt
1	cup chopped nuts
4	cups thinly sliced or grated apples

Apple season is the best time for this cake when apples are really crisp and flavorful. We use Granny Smith apples which have a nice tart taste for baking. Preheat oven to 350°. Grease a 9 × 13 inch pan. Beat the eggs until foamy; then add the oil and mix well. Add sugar, vanilla, spices, soda, flour and salt, mixing after each. Stir in the nuts and apples. Bake for 45 minutes to one hour.

Frosting:

1	(8 ounce) package cream cheese, softened
3	tablespoons butter, softened
2	cups powdered sugar, sifted Few drops of lemon juice
1	teaspoon vanilla

Cream the ingredients and spread on the cooled cake.

Yield: 16 servings

Swedish Apple Nut Pie

Preheat oven to 350°. Butter a 9 inch pie plate. Sift together flour, baking powder, salt and spices. Melt the butter and cool. Beat the egg and add the sugars gradually. Add butter and vanilla and mix well. Add the flour mixture gradually. Fold in apples and nuts and turn into pie plate. Bake for 35 minutes. Serve warm with whipped cream or ice cream.

Yield: 6 servings

½ cup sifted flour
1 teaspoon baking powder
¼ teaspoon salt
¼ teaspoon cinnamon
⅛ teaspoon each clove and nutmeg
1 tablespoon melted butter
1 egg
¼ cup sugar
½ cup light brown sugar, packed
1 teaspoon vanilla
1 cup peeled, chopped apples
½ cup chopped pecans or walnuts

Carrot Cake

2	cups flour
2	cups sugar
2	teaspoons cinnamon
2	teaspoons soda
1⅓	cups salad oil
4	eggs
2	cups grated carrots
1	cup chopped pecans

Preheat oven to 350°. Grease a large tube pan or a 9×13 inch pan. Sift flour, sugar, cinnamon and soda into a mixing bowl. Stir in oil. Add eggs one at a time, beating after each addition. Stir in carrots and pecans. Pour batter into prepared pan. Bake for 1 hour and 20 minutes if using a tube pan, for 45 minutes to an hour for the 9×13 inch pan. Cool. Frost with cream cheese frosting.

Cream Cheese Frosting:

1	(8 ounce) package cream cheese, softened
1	(3 ounce) package cream cheese, softened
¼	cup butter, softened
1	teaspoon vanilla
½	teaspoon lemon juice
2½	cups powdered sugar, sifted

Mix cream cheese, butter, vanilla and lemon juice until well combined. Stir in powdered sugar and beat until smooth. Makes enough frosting for a large tube cake.

Yield: 16 servings

Pineapple Carrot Cake

Preheat oven to 350°. Generously grease a 9 × 13 inch pan. Combine sugar, oil, eggs and vanilla in a mixing bowl, beating at low speed for a minute or two. Add flour, cinnamon, soda and salt and mix well. Fold in carrot, coconut, pineapple and nuts. Pour into pan. Bake for about 50 minutes, until cake tester comes out clean. Cool for 5 minutes and invert onto rack.

2	*cups sugar*
1½	*cups vegetable oil*
3	*eggs*
2	*teaspoons vanilla*
2¼	*cups flour*
2	*teaspoons cinnamon*
2	*teaspoons baking soda*
½	*teaspoon salt*
2	*cups shredded carrot*
2	*cups flaked coconut*
1	*(8 ounce) can crushed pineapple, drained*
1	*cup chopped walnuts or pecans (optional)*

Frosting:

Combine cheese, butter, milk and vanilla, beating well. Then beat in enough sugar to make the frosting spreadable. Frost top and sides of cooled cake.

Yield: 16 servings

6	*ounces cream cheese, softened*
1	*stick butter, melted*
¼	*cup milk*
2	*teaspoons vanilla*
	3 to 4 cups powdered sugar, sifted

127

Clarendon, Texas Pineapple Cake

So named because the recipe was brought to me straight from Clarendon. Georgann and Don Turlington sampled it at a truckstop on their way to Colorado. They liked it so much that they stopped again on their way home to have some more and get the recipe. Thanks for sharing it.

2	**cups flour**
1½	**cups sugar**
2	**teaspoons soda**
1	**(20 ounce) can crushed pineapple and juice**
¾	**cup brown sugar**
¾	**cup chopped pecans**

Preheat oven to 350°. Grease a 12 × 16 inch jelly roll pan. Mix the flour, sugar, soda and pineapple. Pour into pan. Sprinkle the brown sugar and pecans on top and bake for 30 minutes.

Topping:

¾	**cup sugar**
1	**stick butter or margarine**
⅔	**cup evaporated milk**
1	**teaspoon vanilla**

For the topping, mix all the ingredients and cook over medium heat, stirring, for ten minutes. Pour over the hot cake.

Yield: 24 servings

Pineapple Cake

According to my sources, this recipe originated at Neiman Marcus, Dallas, and, like a lot of their merchandise, it is wonderfully rich.

Preheat oven to 350°. Grease and flour a 9 × 13 inch pan. Mix all ingredients and pour into prepared pan. Bake for 35 minutes in the middle of the oven.

2	*cups sugar*
2	*cups flour*
2	*eggs, beaten*
2	*teaspoons soda*
1/8	*teaspoon salt*
1	*teaspoon vanilla*
1	*(20 ounce) can crushed pineapple and juice*
1/2	*cup chopped walnuts or pecans*

Icing:

Mix ingredients well and spread on warm cake.

Yield: 16 servings

8	*ounces cream cheese, softened*
1/2	*stick butter, softened*
2	*cups powdered sugar*
1	*teaspoon vanilla*
1/4	*cup chopped nuts (optional)*
	Coconut (optional)

Italian Cream Cake

How this cake got its name I do not know. Neither does Bon Appetit Magazine where I found the recipe.

	Butter
	Flour
2	**sticks butter, softened**
2	**cups sugar**
5	**eggs**
2	**cups flour**
1	**teaspoon baking soda**
1	**cup buttermilk**
1	**cup flaked coconut**
1	**cup chopped pecans (optional)**
1	**teaspoon vanilla**

Preheat oven to 350°. Butter and flour one 9 × 13 inch pan or three 9 inch cake pans. Cream butter and sugar. Beat in eggs one at a time. Sift dry ingredients and blend into butter mixture. Mix in buttermilk, coconut, pecans and vanilla. Bake for 30 minutes. Test with cake tester. If using 9 inch cake pans, invert onto racks and cool.

Cream Frosting

1	**(8 ounce) package cream cheese, softened**
½	**stick butter, softened**
2	**cups powdered sugar, sifted**
1	**cup chopped pecans (optional)**

Beat cream cheese and butter until well blended. Mix in powdered sugar. Spread over cake. Sprinkle with pecans if desired.

Yield: 16 servings

Pistachio Cream

We don't serve this one anymore because we no longer have space to refrigerate as much as we need to accommodate our growing clientele. It's easy and it's so good.

Mix flour, pecans, and butter well and pat into a buttered 9 × 13 inch pan. Bake at 350° for thirty minutes. Mix cream cheese, powdered sugar and Cool Whip and spread over the crust. Top with pudding mixed with milk as directed on package. You may substitute any flavor of pudding. Chill. Top with remaining Cool Whip flavored with rum or Amaretto.

Yield: 16 servings

1½ cups flour
1½ cups pecans, slightly ground
1½ sticks butter
16   ounces cream cheese, softened
1½ cups powdered sugar
½   large tub of Cool Whip
1   (6 ounce) package instant pistachio pudding

Chocolate Pound Cake

2	sticks butter
½	cup Crisco shortening
3	cups sugar
5	eggs
3	cups cake flour
½	cup cocoa
½	teaspoon baking powder
½	teaspoon salt
1	cup milk
2	teaspoons Mexican vanilla

Preheat the oven to 325°. Carefully grease and flour a Bundt pan. Cream butter, Crisco and sugar. Add the eggs one at a time. Combine flour, cocoa, baking powder and salt. Mix half of the dry ingredients into the sugar mixture. Add half of the milk and vanilla and then remaining flour, followed by remaining milk. Bake for 1 hour. Cool and remove from pan. We serve it with chocolate sauce and whipped cream flavored with Myers's rum.

Yield: 16 servings

German Chocolate Pound Cake

4	ounces German's sweet chocolate, melted
2	cups sugar
1	cup shortening
4	eggs
2	teaspoons vanilla
2	teaspoons butter flavoring*
1	cup buttermilk
3	cups sifted flour
½	teaspoon baking soda
1	teaspoon salt

Preheat oven to 300°. Grease and flour a Bundt pan. Cream sugar and shortening. Add eggs, flavoring and buttermilk. Sift flour with soda and salt and add to sugar and shortening, mixing well. Blend in chocolate. Pour into prepared pan and bake for one hour and 30 minutes. Remove from pan while warm and top with the following glaze.

*Or you may omit the butter flavor and substitute 1 cup of butter for the shortening.

Glaze:

4	ounces German's sweet chocolate
1	tablespoon butter
¼	cup water
1	cup sifted powdered sugar
½	teaspoon vanilla

Melt butter and chocolate over low heat. Mix sugar and salt and blend in chocolate and vanilla. For a thinner glaze, add more hot water.

Yield: 16 servings

Chocolate Zucchini Cake

If zucchini can go into bread, why not cake? Like the bread, zucchini cake is wonderfully moist. It is a must for all chocolate lovers.

Preheat oven to 325°. Grease and flour a Bundt pan. Combine dry ingredients. Cream shortening and butter with sugar until light and fluffy. Add eggs one at a time, beating after each addition. Alternately add dry ingredients, milk and zucchini, mixing well. Add vanilla. Pour into prepared pan and sprinkle with chocolate morsels which have been mixed with the 2 tablespoons of sugar. Bake for about 50 minutes. Allow to cool for 10 minutes and invert onto serving platter. Serve with fresh raspberries or strawberries and whipped cream flavored with Kahlua.

Yield: 16

2½	*cups flour*
½	*teaspoon baking powder*
1	*teaspoon baking soda*
4	*tablespoons cocoa*
¼	*teaspoon ground cloves*
½	*teaspoon cinnamon*
½	*cup shortening*
½	*cup butter or margarine, softened*
1¾	*cups sugar*
3	*eggs*
½	*cup buttermilk*
1	*teaspoon vanilla*
2	*cups peeled and grated zucchini*
¼	*cup semisweet chocolate morsels*
2	*tablespoons sugar*

Lemon Pound Cake

3	*sticks butter*
2⅔	*cups sugar*
5	*eggs*
3	*cups cake flour*
1	*teaspoon baking powder*
½	*teaspoon salt*
1	*cup milk*
2	*tablespoons lemon extract, almond extract, Amaretto, or other flavoring*

Preheat oven to 325°. Grease and flour a Bundt pan. Cream together butter and sugar until light and fluffy. Add eggs one at a time. Mix in dry ingredients alternately with milk. Add flavoring. Pour into prepared pan and bake for 1 hour. Cool on a rack for five minutes and turn out onto serving platter.

Yield: 16 servings

7-Up Cake

2	*sticks butter*
3	*cups sugar*
½	*cup Crisco oil*
5	*large eggs*
2	*teaspoons lemon extract*
3	*cups flour*
1	*cup 7-Up*

Preheat oven to 325°. Grease and flour a Bundt pan. Cream butter, sugar, and oil. Add eggs one at a time, beating after each. Add lemon extract. Alternately add flour and 7-Up. Pour into prepared pan and bake for 50 minutes to 1 hour.

Yield: 16 servings

Pineapple Pound Cake

Mrs. John Roberson of Smithfield submitted this recipe to the Star Telegram in 1973. Georgann Turlington cut it out and passed it along to me. Everyone loves it.

Grease and flour a Bundt pan. Cream shortening, butter and sugar until fluffy. Add eggs one at a time, beating thoroughly after each addition. Add dry ingredients alternately with milk. Add vanilla and stir in pineapple, blending well. Pour into Bundt pan. Place in cold oven. Turn on oven to 325° and bake for 1½ hours. Let cool for 5 minutes. Turn out of pan.

½	cup shortening
2	sticks butter
2¾	cups sugar
6	eggs
3	cups flour
1	teaspoon baking powder
½	cup milk
1	teaspoon vanilla
1	cup undrained crushed pineapple

Glaze:

Combine and drizzle over cool cake.

Yield: 16 servings

½	stick butter
2	cups powdered sugar
¼	cup pineapple juice

Coconut Pound Cake

Thanks to Marlene Wood, a fellow student at the French Apron, for this luscious coconut concoction.

Preheat oven to 325°. Grease and flour a Bundt pan. Cream together the butter and sugar until light and fluffy. Add flour and eggs alternately, mixing well. Beat in remaining ingredients. Pour into prepared pan and bake for about 1 hour. Test for doneness with a cake tester. Cool on a rack for five minutes and turn out onto serving platter.

Yield: 16 servings

3	sticks butter
3	cups sugar
3	cups flour
6	eggs
1	cup sour cream
1	teaspoon vanilla
1	teaspoon coconut flavoring
¼	teaspoon baking soda
1	cup coconut flakes

Rum Cake

Rum cake keeps almost forever and freezes well, making a nice gift.

1	*box yellow cake mix*
1	*small package instant vanilla pudding*
4	*eggs*
½	*cup salad oil*
½	*cup water*
½	*cup Myers's rum*
1	*cup broken pecan pieces*

Preheat oven to 325°. Grease and flour a Bundt pan. Beat all ingredients together, except nuts for 7 to 8 minutes. Fold nuts into batter. Pour batter into pan and bake for 45 minutes to 1 hour. Test with cake tester. Remove from oven. Just as you remove the cake, begin the topping.

Topping:

1	*cup sugar*
1	*stick butter*
¼	*cup water*
¼	*cup Myers's rum*

Boil sugar, water, butter for two minutes, stirring so that the mixture will not boil over. Add rum, mixing well. Ladle hot mixture over hot cake (still in the pan). Let cake cool until all liquid is absorbed. Turn out onto serving platter. Serve with vanilla ice cream or whipped cream.

Yield: 16 servings

Sock-It-To-Me Cake

My longtime carpool comrade, Toni Mann, gave me this rich concoction. It makes a good coffee cake also.

Preheat oven to 350°. Grease and flour a Bundt pan. Mix all ingredients well. Spoon ½ of batter into pan. Sprinkle ½ of cinnamon mixture over batter. Spread remaining batter over this; then sprinkle remainder of cinnamon mixture on top. Bake for 45 minutes to 1 hour. Cool in pan for 5 minutes. This cake is wonderful served warm with some whipped cream. It can be frozen.

Yield: 16 servings

1⅔	sticks butter at room temperature
2	cups sugar
2	eggs
1	cup sour cream
2	cups flour
1½	teaspoons baking powder
¼	teaspoon salt
½	teaspoon vanilla or Mexican vanilla
¾	teaspoon nutmeg

Cinnamon mixture

½	cup chopped nuts
¼	cup packed brown sugar
1	teaspoon cinnamon

Ollie's Pie Crust

Ollie Milton, our other veteran baker, is well known for her wonderful pies. We had a time coming up with this one because Ollie only knows how to make 16 crusts at once. But perseverance paid off and here it is.

3	**cups flour**
1	**cup Crisco (a must)**
1	**teaspoon salt**
½	**cup water**

Mix flour, Crisco and salt with your fingers until it resembles coarse meal. Gradually sprinkle water and mix until you have a ball. Press dough into a flat circle with smooth edges. On a cool, lightly floured surface, roll dough into a circle, rolling to the edges from the center. Turn dough and repeat this process until you have a nice, round circle about 1½ inches larger than the inverted pie plate. Carefully fold dough in half and ease it into the pie plate. Try not to stretch the dough or it will shrink badly. Crimp the edges with thumb and forefinger; then trim with a knife.

Tip: The crust may be frozen, wrapped in foil in the pie plate, or left in the ball to be rolled out at another time.

Yield: 3-4 crusts

Baked Pie Crust

Preheat oven to 400°. Prick bottom and sides of pie crust. To prevent shrinking, set another pie plate of the same dimension inside the crust or line crust with foil and add enough "pie weights" or dried beans to cover the bottom. Bake for 10 minutes. Remove pie plate or beans. Return to oven and continue baking for another 10 minutes or until crust is as brown as you desire.

Pecan Pie

4	large eggs
1	tablespoon flour
¾	cup sugar
1¼	cups light Karo
	Pinch salt
1	tablespoon vanilla
1½	cups pecans
⅓	cup melted butter
1	teaspoon lemon extract
	A 9" unbaked pie shell

Preheat oven to 400°. Beat the eggs. Mix flour and sugar and add gradually to the eggs. Add remaining ingredients in order. Pour into pie shell (do not prick the bottom). Bake at 400° for 10 minutes, then lower the temperature to 350° and bake for 50 minutes more.

Yield: 8 servings

Raisin Pecan Pie

I had never even heard of Raisin Pie when one of our staff asked me if we could make it. As if by magic, Georgann Turlington came in with this recipe the next day.

2	cups sugar
4	eggs
1	stick butter, room temperature
2	tablespoons vinegar
1	cup raisins
1	cup chopped pecans
	A 9" unbaked pie shell

Preheat oven to 375°. Mix all together. Pour into pie shell and bake at 375° for 25 to 30 minutes. Turn oven down to 350° and bake for another 30 minutes. Serve with whipped cream or ice cream.

Yield: 8 servings

Chocolate Pecan Pie

Strictly for chocolate lovers.

Preheat oven to 350°. Cream the butter and sugar until light. Add eggs, one at a time, beating well after each addition. Add salt, vanilla, bourbon, corn syrup, molasses, and blend well. Sprinkle flour over nuts; then add nuts and chocolate chips to the filling and pour into pie shell. Bake for 35 minutes. Serve with whipped cream flavored with vanilla, bourbon or Kahlua.

Yield: 8 servings

1	*stick unsalted butter*
⅔	*cup lightly packed brown sugar*
3	*eggs*
¼	*teaspoon salt*
1	*teaspoon vanilla*
1	*tablespoon bourbon or rum*
½	*cup corn syrup*
3	*tablespoons molasses*
1	*heaping tablespoon flour*
1⅓	*cups pecan pieces*
½	*cup semi-sweet chocolate chips*
½	*cup whipping cream*
	A 9″ unbaked pie shell

Brownie Pie

1	*(1 ounce) square unsweetened chocolate*
2	*sticks butter*
1	*cup sugar*
½	*cup flour*
2	*eggs*
1	*teaspoon vanilla*
½	*cup chopped pecans*
	A 9" unbaked pie shell

Preheat oven to 375°. Melt chocolate in a double boiler. Set aside to cool. Cream butter and sugar until fluffy. Blend in flour, eggs, vanilla and cooled chocolate. Stir in pecans. Pour into pie shell and bake for 25 minutes. Top with whipped cream or your favorite ice cream.

Yield: 8 servings

Toll House Pie

A slice of this pie is like a big moist chocolate chip cookie. Top with whipped cream or ice cream and you have got a wonderful dessert. The recipe comes right from the Nestle Company.

2	*eggs*
½	*cup flour*
½	*cup sugar*
½	*cup packed brown sugar*
1	*cup butter, melted and cooled to room temperature*
1	*(6 ounce) package semi-sweet chocolate morsels*
1	*cup chopped nuts*
	A 9" unbaked pie shell

Preheat oven to 325°. In a large bowl, beat eggs until foamy. Add flour, sugar, brown sugar and beat until blended. Stir in melted butter. Fold in chocolate morsels and nuts. Spread in the pie shell. Bake at 325° for one hour. Remove from oven and serve warm with whipped cream or ice cream.

The recipe may be doubled. Bake two pies and freeze one for later use.

Yield: 8 servings

Chocolate Chess Pie

Preheat oven to 350°. Mix sugar, meal, and cocoa. Combine eggs, butter, corn syrup and vanilla. Pour egg mixture into dry ingredients and stir until there are no lumps. Pour into pie shell and bake for 45 minutes, or until filling has set and a knife inserted in the center comes out clean.

1	*cup sugar*
3	*tablespoons cornmeal*
3	*tablespoons cocoa*
3	*eggs, well beaten*
1	*stick butter, melted*
½	*cup light corn syrup*
1	*teaspoon vanilla*
	A 9" unbaked pie shell

Yield: 8 servings

Chess Pie

One of the best memories of my childhood was my grandmother's chess pie. So I decided to serve it at The Buffet until I realized that we would need 100 egg yolks per day to make enough pies. What would we do with all the whites?

Preheat oven to 375°. Beat the yolks well and gradually add sugar, beating until mixture is light and creamy. Add butter and cream, combining well. Pour batter into pie shell and bake for 30 to 40 minutes until the custard is set.

8	*egg yolks*
1	*cup sugar*
2	*tablespoons melted butter*
1	*cup whipping cream*
	Dash salt
	Dash nutmeg
	A 9" unbaked pie shell

Yield: 8 servings

Buttermilk Pie

1¼   *cups sugar*
2   *tablespoons flour*
½   *stick butter, softened*
3   *eggs*
2   *cups buttermilk*
⅛   *teaspoon salt*
1   *tablespoon vanilla*
  A 9" unbaked pie shell

Preheat oven to 400°. Combine sugar, flour and butter and beat until smooth. Add eggs one at a time, beating well after each. Stir in buttermilk, salt and vanilla. Pour into pie shell. Bake at 400° for 10 minutes; reduce temperature to 350° and bake for another 40 minutes until filling is set and lightly brown. Whipped cream is good with this too. In fact, a little whipped cream is good with almost everything. Some sliced strawberries would make the plate colorful.

Yield: 8 servings

Lemon Pie

3   *eggs, separated*
1   *cup sugar*
½   *stick butter, softened*
1   *cup milk*
1   *tablespoon flour*
¼   *cup lemon juice*
1   *tablespoon grated lemon rind*
  A 9" unbaked pie shell

Preheat oven to 350°. Beat the egg whites until stiff, adding ½ of the sugar gradually. Set aside. In another bowl, beat the other half of the sugar with the butter, egg yolks, milk, flour, lemon juice, and grated lemon rind. Fold a little of the egg white into this mixture. Then fold this into the egg white mixture. Pour into pie shell. Bake for 35 to 40 minutes. Serve with Sauce Cardinale.

Yield: 8 servings

Blueberry Pie

Preheat oven to 400°. Wash and pick over fresh berries, or if berries are frozen, thaw and let drain. The amounts of sugar, flour, cornstarch, and lemon juice will vary according to your berries and how sweet, acid, or juicy they are. Lightly toss all the ingredients and pour into the pie crust. Then top it, making sure to crimp the edges well. Then brush crust with milk or cream. To avoid a big mess in the bottom of your oven, set the pie on a cookie sheet lined with foil. Bake for 45 to 50 minutes. Top with whipped cream.

Yield: 8 servings

4	cups fresh or frozen blueberries
½ to 1 cup sugar, depending upon the sweetness of the fruit
4	tablespoons flour
2	teaspoons cornstarch
1½	teaspoons lemon juice
1	tablespoon unsalted butter, melted
	A 9" double pie crust
	Milk or cream to brush pie crust

Key Lime Pie

I got this recipe from the Driskill Hotel in Austin after a wonderful dinner there many years ago. Key limes are the small ones from the Florida Keys. They have the best flavor; but if you can't find them, any lime will do.

Beat egg yolks, gradually add milk and lime juice. In another bowl, beat egg whites until light and fluffy. Fold a little of the egg whites into the yolks to lighten the mixture. Then fold the yolk mixture into the remaining whites. Spoon mixture into crust and freeze pie for 24 hours.

Top with whipped cream flavored with a little sugar and dark rum and coconut if you like it.

Yield: 8 servings

2	eggs, separated
1	(14 ounce) can Eagle Brand milk
½	cup fresh lime juice
	A 9" graham cracker crumb crust

Cherry Pie

1	*cup sugar*
¼	*cup flour or 2 tablespoons cornstarch*
3	*cups pie cherries, drained*
½	*stick butter*
1	*teaspoon almond extract*
	A 9" double pie crust
	Milk or cream to brush pie crust

Preheat oven to 400°. Combine ingredients gently without doing too much damage to the cherries. Pour into pie shell. Cover with another crust or a lattice. Brush crust with milk or cream. Bake until nicely browned, about 45 minutes.

Yield: 8 servings

Apple Pie

1	*cup sugar*
1	*tablespoon flour*
½	*teaspoon cinnamon*
⅛	*teaspoon nutmeg*
5	*cups Granny Smith apples, peeled, cored and thinly sliced*
1½	*tablespoons butter*
	Milk to brush pie crust
	Lemon juice if the apples are not very tasty
	A 9" double pie crust

Preheat oven to 400°. Mix the dry ingredients. Toss with the apples, pour into pie shell and dot with butter. Cover with a whole crust or a lattice. Brush crust with milk. Bake for 30 to 40 minutes until pie is nicely browned.

Yield: 8 servings

Sour Cream Apple Pie

Preheat oven to 350°. Combine flour
and sugar. Add egg, sour cream,
vanilla, and salt. Beat until smooth.
Fold in the apples and pour into the
pie shell.

2	*tablespoons flour*
1	*cup sugar*
1	*egg slightly beaten*
1	*cup sour cream*
1	*teaspoon vanilla*
¼	*teaspoon salt*
5	*cups Granny Smith apples, peeled, cored and thinly sliced*
	A 9″ unbaked pie shell

Topping:

For the topping, blend sugar, flour
and butter until crumbly. Cover the
pie with this mixture. Bake for 30
minutes.

Yield: 8 servings

½	*cup sugar*
5	*tablespoons flour*
½	*stick butter*

Apricot Pie

1	*(1 pound 13 ounce) can of apricot halves, drained, or an equal amount of fresh apricots*
1	*tablespoon lemon juice*
	A 9" unbaked pie shell

Preheat oven to 400°. Toss apricots with lemon juice. Spread in pie shell.

Topping:

½	*cup flour*
¾	*cup sugar*
¼	*teaspoon cinnamon*
¼	*teaspoon nutmeg*
½	*stick butter, softened*

For the topping, mix dry ingredients and butter with your fingers until mixture resembles coarse meal. Sprinkle over apricots. Bake for 40 to 45 minutes until crust and top are golden brown. Serve with whipped cream or ice cream. I would love it with pistachio ice cream.

Yield: 8 servings

Peach Pie

Preheat oven to 350°. Toss peaches with lemon juice. Mix dry ingredients and toss with the peaches. Pour into pie shell, dot with butter, and top with crust or the following topping:

1	*(1 lb. 13 oz.) can sliced peaches, drained or an equal amount of fresh peaches, peeled and sliced (about 5-6 cups)*
1	*teaspoon fresh lemon juice*
¾-1	*cup sugar*
¼	*cup flour*
¼	*teaspoon nutmeg*
2	*tablespoons butter*
	A 9" unbaked pie shell

Almond Topping

Put all ingredients in a processor. Pulse several times to mix. Top pie completely. Bake for 40 to 50 minutes.

Note: this topping is good on any fruit pie.

Yield: 8 servings

¾	*cup flour*
6	*tablespoons sugar*
6	*tablespoons unsalted butter*
½	*cup slivered almonds*

Chocolate Pie

Unfortunately, we can't serve custard pies due to a refrigerated space problem. If we could, this chocolate pie of Ollie's would be tops on my list.

1½ **cups sugar**
⅓   **cup cornstarch**
½   **teaspoon salt**
3   **cups milk**
4   **egg yolks, beaten**
2   **ounces baking chocolate**
1   **tablespoon and 1 teaspoon vanilla—I would like Mexican vanilla**
    A 9″ baked pie shell

Combine sugar, cornstarch and salt. Add a little milk to cornstarch mixture, stirring to combine, then add remaining milk and egg yolks, stirring well. Add chocolate. Cook over low heat or in a double boiler. Stir with a whip until the custard is thick. Don't try to rush this or you'll have some very sweet scrambled eggs. Remove from heat and add vanilla. Pour in the pie shell, chill and top with whipped cream.

Yield: 8 servings

Pineapple Cream Cheese Pie

Preheat oven to 400°. In a saucepan combine sugar, cornstarch and pineapple. Cook, stirring, until thick. Set aside to cool.

For topping, cream sugar, salt and cream cheese, until fluffy. Blend in remaining ingredients except nuts.

Spread cooled pineapple in pie shell. Top with cream cheese mixture. Sprinkle with nuts if desired. Bake at 400° for 10 minutes; reduce heat to 325° and continue baking for 50 minutes until golden on top.

Yield: 8 servings

⅓ *cup sugar*
1 *tablespoon cornstarch*
  A 9 ounce can crushed pineapple

Topping:

½ *cup sugar*
½ *teaspoon salt*
2 *(8 ounce) packages cream cheese, softened*
2 *eggs*
½ *cup milk*
½ *teaspoon vanilla*
¼ *cup chopped nuts (optional)*
  A 9″ unbaked pie shell

Coconut Cream Pie

¼	*cup cornstarch*
⅔	*cup sugar*
½	*teaspoon salt*
3	*cups milk*
4	*egg yolks, beaten*
¾	*cup coconut*
2	*tablespoons butter*
1	*tablespoon plus 1 teaspoon vanilla*
	A 9" baked pie shell

Combine cornstarch, sugar and salt. Add milk and egg yolks. Cook over low heat, being careful not to scramble the eggs, until the custard is thick. Remove from heat and cool. Stir in the coconut, butter and vanilla. Pour into pie shell. Top with whipped cream and toasted coconut.

Yield: 8 servings

Sweet Potato Pie

Even people who don't like sweet potatoes like this pie.

Preheat oven to 375°. Cook sweet potatoes in their jackets in boiling water for about 30 minutes until they are tender. Let the sweet potatoes cool and peel them. Coarsely chop them and combine with remaining ingredients. With the steel blade of a food processor, blend the mixture in batches until light and fluffy. Pour into pie shell and bake for 25 to 30 minutes.

Yield: 8 servings

3   *medium sweet potatoes*
1½ *cups sugar*
1   *teaspoon vanilla*
1   *teaspoon nutmeg*
     A pinch of cinnamon
1   *stick butter, melted*
1   *cup Carnation evaporated milk*
2   *eggs, beaten*
     A 9" unbaked pie shell

Lemon Almond Squares

Here is a variation on the theme for those who love almonds and chocolate. It has been adapted for the food processor but can be made like Lemon Squares (page 155).

Crust:

3	tablespoons almonds
1¼	cup flour
1½	sticks well-chilled unsalted butter, cut into 12 pieces
6	tablespoons powdered sugar
¾	teaspoon lemon extract
⅛	teaspoon salt

Preheat oven to 375°. Grease a 9 × 13 inch pan. You may use Pam if you prefer. In a food processor, with the steel knife, mince the almonds, using on/off turns. Add flour and process about 1 minute. Add remaining crust ingredients and combine with on/off turns. Process until dough begins to mass together, about 5 seconds. Pat into the bottom of the pan and bake for about 10 minutes, or until lightly golden.

Topping:

1	cup and 2 tablespoons sugar Zest of 1 lemon
3	large eggs
3¾	tablespoons flour
1½	teaspoon lemon extract
¾	teaspoon baking powder Pinch of salt
2	ounces semisweet chocolate, chopped with steel blade
⅜	cup toasted, sliced almonds

While crust is baking, prepare topping. In the processor, using the steel knife again, combine half of the sugar and the lemon zest until zest is finely minced, about 1 minute. Add remaining sugar and eggs and process 30 seconds until thick and light colored. Add remaining ingredients except chocolate and almonds, and process another 30 seconds.

When crust is golden, remove from oven and reduce heat to 350°. Sprinkle crust with chopped chocolate at this point. Pour topping over curst and sprinkle with almonds. Bake for another 25 minutes. Cool before cutting into squares using wet knife method.

Yield: 16-24 squares

Lemon Squares

A recipe that has been around a long time—and rightfully so. They are delicious.

Preheat oven to 325°. Mix butter, flour and powdered sugar and press into a 9×13 inch pan. Bake for 15 minutes.

2	*sticks unsalted butter*
2	*cups flour*
½	*cup powdered sugar*

Topping:

Beat the eggs slightly. Add sugar, lemon juice, flour, baking powder and pecans, if desired. Mix well and pour on top of the pastry. Bake at 325° for 40 to 50 minutes. Sprinkle with additional powdered sugar if you like. Cool and cut into squares with a sharp, wet knife. Keep wiping off the knife so that the custard won't stick so badly.

Yield: 16-24 squares

4	*eggs*
2	*cups sugar*
6	*tablespoons lemon juice*
1	*tablespoon flour*
½	*teaspoon baking powder*
1	*cup finely chopped pecans (optional)*

Brownies

2	*(1 ounce) squares baking chocolate*
1	*stick butter*
2	*eggs*
1	*cup sugar*
½	*cup flour*
	Dash of salt
1	*teaspoon vanilla*
½	*cup chopped pecans*
1	*(6 ounce) package of semi-sweet chocolate chips*

Preheat oven to 325°. Grease a 9x9 inch pan. Melt chocolate and butter over low heat and set aside to cool. Beat eggs and stir in sugar gradually. Add chocolate and butter mixture and mix well. Add flour, salt and vanilla, beating until combined. Fold in pecans and chocolate morsels. Spread in pan and bake for 25 to 30 minutes. Sometimes we use chocolate frosting to top the brownies. Vanilla ice cream with raspberry or strawberry sauce is excellent also.

Yield: 9-12 squares

Pan Tollhouse Cookies

Need cookies for a group in a hurry? This recipe fills a half sheet, available at restaurant supply stores or two 9×13 inch pans.

4½	*cups flour*
2	*teaspoons soda*
2	*teaspoons salt*
4	*sticks butter, softened*
1½	*cups sugar*
1½	*cups brown sugar, packed*
4	*eggs*
2	*teaspoons vanilla*
2	*(12 ounce) packages semisweet chocolate chips*
2	*cups chopped nuts*

Preheat oven to 350°. Lightly grease pan. Combine flour, soda and salt in a bowl. Cream butter and sugars until fluffy. Add eggs and vanilla and mix well. Slowly add flour mixture, continuing mixing until well combined. Stir in chips and nuts. Spread into pan and bake for 30 minutes.

Yield: 24-36 cookies

Cream Cheese Brownies

Preheat oven to 350°. Grease an 8 or 9 inch square pan. Melt chocolate and butter over very low heat. Set aside to cool.

For the cream cheese batter, blend butter and cream cheese. Gradually add sugar beating well. Stir in egg, flour and vanilla. Set aside.

For the chocolate batter, beat eggs until thick and light in color, slowly add sugar, beating well. Add baking powder, salt and flour. Stir in melted chocolate mixture, nuts, vanilla and almond extract. Spread about half of the chocolate batter in the pan. Add cheese mixture, spreading evenly. Top with spoonfuls of chocolate batter. Zigzag with a spatula to marble. Bake for 35 to 40 minutes.

Yield: 16 squares

4	*ounces German's sweet chocolate*
3	*tablespoons butter or margarine*

Cream Cheese Batter:

2	*tablespoons butter or margarine*
3	*ounces cream cheese, softened*
¼	*cup sugar*
1	*egg*
1	*tablespoon flour*
½	*teaspoon vanilla*

Chocolate Batter:

2	*eggs*
¾	*cup sugar*
½	*teaspoon baking powder*
¼	*teaspoon salt*
½	*cup flour*
½	*cup chopped nuts*
1	*teaspoon vanilla*
¼	*teaspoon almond extract*

Pecan Bars

This recipe is my mother's. Pecan bars are great with a scoop of bourbon ice cream and chocolate sauce.

2	*tablespoons butter*
5	*tablespoons flour*
⅛	*teaspoon baking soda*
1	*cup chopped pecans*
2	*eggs*
¾	*teaspoon vanilla*
¼	*teaspoon lemon extract*
1	*cup brown sugar, packed*

Preheat oven to 350°. Melt butter in an 8×8 inch pan and set aside. Combine flour, soda and nuts. In a mixer, beat the eggs and vanilla and lemon extract until thick. Gradually add sugar and beat well. Add dry ingredients and mix. Spread in buttered pan. Bake for 25 minutes. While warm, cut into squares.

Yield: 9-12 squares

Gingerbread

Preheat oven to 350°. Grease and flour a 9×9 inch pan. Sift dry ingredients into mixing bowl. Add egg, sugar and molasses and mix well. Pour boiling water into oil and add slowly to other ingredients. Pour into prepared pan. Bake for 35 to 40 minutes. Serve warm, topped with lemon sauce or whipped cream or both.

Yield: 9-12 servings

1⅔   cups flour
1¼   teaspoons soda
1½   teaspoons ginger
¾   teaspoon cinnamon
¾   teaspoon salt
1   egg, beaten
½   cup sugar
½   cup molasses
½   boiling water
½   cup oil

DESSERTS

World's Best Cookies

2	sticks butter, softened
1	cup sugar
1	cup brown sugar, packed
1	egg
1	cup oil
1	cup oats
2	cups cornflakes, crushed to make 1 cup
½	cup coconut
3½	cups flour
1	teaspoon soda
1	teaspoon salt
1	teaspoon vanilla
½	cup pecan pieces

Peheat oven to 350°. Cream the butter and sugars. Add egg and mix well. Add the remaining ingredients, beating well after each addition. Drop by the spoonful onto a cookie sheet and press with a fork. Bake for 12 minutes. Remove from cookie sheet and sprinkle with sugar. These cookies freeze very well.

Yield: 90-100 2″ cookies

Whipped Cream

The secrets to light fluffy whipped cream are cold cream and cold equipment. Whip cream in a mixer or a food processor. When it has begun to thicken, add the sugar and vanilla. Some other flavorings are: rum, créme de cocoa, Kahlua, créme de menthe, etc.

Yield: 1½ cups

1   cup whipping cream
2   tablespoons sugar
½   teaspoon vanilla or other flavoring

Honey Whipped Cream

Beat well-chilled cream in mixer or food processor. Add honey slowly. When cream is thick, beat in cognac.

Yield: 1½ cups

1   cup whipping cream
1   tablespoon honey
½   teaspoon cognac

Blueberry Sauce

¾	cup sugar
1½	tablespoons cornstarch
¾	cup water
¼	teaspoon lemon extract
1	pint fresh blueberries
	A dash of crème de cassis, Cointreau or other liqueur (optional)

Mix sugar and cornstarch in warm water, stirring to dissolve. Bring to a boil and cook stirring for 5 minutes. Add remaining ingredients and simmer until berries begin to fall apart, about 15 minutes. Make lots of sauce while fresh berries are available and freeze for later use.

Yield: 2-3 cups

Sauce Cardinale

Buy berries in the height of berry season, make the sauce and freeze it for use the next winter.

1	cup puréed strawberries
1	cup puréed raspberries
1	cup sugar
1	teaspoon cornstarch

Mix ingredients well in a saucepan. Bring to a boil and cook until thickened. Cool and run through a sieve.

Yield: 2 cups

Lemon Sauce a la Helen Corbitt

Mix sugar, salt and cornstarch; add boiling water and cook until clear; add lemon rind and continue cooking 1 minute. Remove from heat and stir in butter and lemon juice. Serve hot. Adding the lemon juice after removing from heat gives the fresh taste you should desire.

Helen Corbitt adds: "Orange sauce, equally popular, I use over baked custards, substituting orange juice and rind for lemon juice and rind . . . Then add 1 teaspoon lemon juice. You may use Lemon Sauce as a foundation for other fruit sauces but always add the 1 teaspoon of lemon juice to spark its taste."

Yield: 1½ cups

½	*cup sugar*
¼	*teaspoon salt*
1	*tablespoon cornstarch*
1	*cup boiling water*
1	*teaspoon grated lemon rind*
2	*tablespoons butter*
3	*tablespoons lemon juice*

APPETIZERS

Entertaining in your home can be as simple or as difficult as you choose to make it. Home entertaining need not be a monumental task. It does require a bit of organization. One of the best books I have read on the subject is *Entertaining,* by Martha Stewart (Clarkson N. Potter, Inc., Publisher, New York, 1982). The book provides both menu and decorating ideas for almost every sort of occasion.

One of the secrets to success is not to get in over your head. If you want to use a new recipe, try it before the day of the party. If you do not have time to prepare everything yourself, find a caterer to fill your need. Many items can be made and frozen well ahead of the event.

A large affair simply requires a bit more time and organization. The recipes in this section have been multiplied to serve as many as 700 guests. If you double or triple a recipe, be careful to add the salt at the end of the preparation. I have provided only cup measurements for these recipes because the number served depends upon how many dishes you plan to serve.

Decorating is the fun part of the preparation. I did not realize that I possessed any creativity until I began presenting food. I have done some very complicated presentations which involve carving vegetables into flowers, and there are books available on the subject if you are interested in that sort of thing. Frequently, your own backyard can be a valuable decorative resource: holly and nandina at Christmas, spring and summer flowers, and autumn leaves. Also, seashells, decorative rocks, swags of material, house plants and, of course, candles lend great decorating flair. An attractive bowl filled with colorful fruits and vegetables provides an unusual centerpiece. I use a lot of cut flowers and greenery for adding a special touch to the food trays. In my opinion, one of the keys to an attractive table is simplicity.

Provençal Mayonnaise

Process all ingredients except 1 tablespoon of capers in a food processor until blended. Fold in capers and refrigerate. This is an unusual dip for vegetables, especially good with artichokes.

Yield: 2 cups

2	*cups Hellman's or homemade mayonnaise*
3	*tablespoons capers*
2	*tablespoons tomato paste*
1	*tablespoon anchovy paste*
1	*teaspoon lemon juice*
	Pinch of tarragon

Ravigote Mayonnaise

I found this recipe in THE PLEASURES OF COOKING, an excellent magazine published by Cuisinart. As you might suspect, all the recipes are designed for the food processor. I sometimes cheat and just chop the first 5 ingredients and add them to two cups of Hellman's with a little lemon juice and Dijon-style mustard.

With the metal blade, process parsley, capers, tarragon, anchovies and cornichon about 2 seconds until minced. I prefer to set this mixture aside and add it to the mayonnaise later; but if you want a smooth mayonnaise, leave it in the processor and continue as follows: Add egg, lemon juice, mustard, salt, pepper and 2 tablespoons of the oil. Process until mixture thickens, about 8 seconds.

With the machine running, drizzle oil through the feed tube, slowly at first and more quickly as mayonnaise begins to thicken. Adjust seasoning.

Yield: 2 cups

2	*tablespoons fresh parsley leaves, loosely packed*
2	*teaspoons capers, drained*
½	*teaspoon dried tarragon*
2	*anchovy fillets, washed and patted dry*
1	*large cornichon or a (1 ounce) piece of dill pickle*
1	*large egg*
1	*tablespoon lemon juice*
1	*teaspoon Dijon-style mustard*
¼	*teaspoon salt*
	Freshly ground pepper
1½	*cups vegetable or olive oil*

APPETIZERS

Artichoke and Spinach Dip

2	*(8½ ounce) cans artichoke hearts or bottoms, drained*
8-10	*ounces fresh spinach, picked over and washed well*
¼	*cup chopped parsley*
3	*tablespoons minced shallot or green onion*
1	*large garlic clove, mashed*
2	*tablespoons fresh lemon juice*
2	*teaspoons dill*
1	*cup Hellman's or homemade mayonnaise*
2	*cups sour cream*
1	*tablespoon Dijon-style mustard*
	Salt and freshly grated pepper
	Buttermilk if desired to thin

Purée artichokes in a food processor. Cook spinach (the water on the leaves provides enough moisture) over medium heat for about 5 minutes. Drain, cool, squeeze dry and chop it. Combine ingredients. Serve with crudités such as asparagus, Belgian endive, snow peas or sliced jicama. We thin the recipe with some buttermilk to serve as a salad dressing.

Yield: 5-6 cups

Artichoke Dip

This recipe is simple and is great doubled for a sizable crowd.

2	*(14 ounce) cans artichoke hearts, drained and chopped fine in a food processor*
8	*ounces grated Parmesan cheese*
1	*pint mayonnaise*
1	*teaspoon garlic powder*
½	*teaspoon basil*
	Juice of one lemon
	Dash of Tabasco

Mix ingredients well in a 2-quart glass dish. Microwave on high for 4 minutes, stirring once during cooking, or heat at 350° in a conventional oven for 20 to 30 minutes until bubbly.

Yield: about 8 cups

NOTE: The mayonnaise will curdle if the dip gets too hot.

Broccoli Shrimp Dip

Of course you could thin this recipe with chicken stock and cream and have soup. Another opportunity for experimenting. You may try Swiss, Jarlsburg, Gouda, or Fontina just to name a few cheeses.

Sauté celery, onion, and mushrooms in butter for 10 minutes. Set aside. Blanch broccoli in 2 quarts boiling salted water for 5 minutes. Drain and refresh with cold water. In a large, heavy saucepan, combine sautéed vegetable mixture with mushroom soup and heat through. Stir in the cheese and continue stirring and cooking until cheese is all melted. Add seasonings. Just before you are ready to serve, stir in the broccoli and shrimp. The dip may be presented in a chafing dish or simply in a bowl surrounded by crackers or melba toast.

Yield: 8 cups

2	*tablespoons butter*
½	*cup chopped celery*
1	*cup minced onion*
1½	*cups chopped mushrooms*
4	*cups chopped broccoli*
2	*(10¾ ounce) cans mushroom soup*
3	*cups (12 ounces) grated sharp Cheddar cheese*
½	*teaspoon garlic powder*
½	*teaspoon season salt*
6	*shakes Tabasco*
¾	*pound cooked shrimp, coarsely chopped*

171

Pickadillo-Almond Dip

½	pound lean ground beef
½	pound lean ground pork
1	teaspoon salt
¼	teaspoon pepper
1	(2 pound) can whole tomatoes, chopped, reserving the juice, or 4 medium tomatoes, peeled and diced
2½	garlic cloves, mashed
1	small onion, chopped
1	(6 ounce) can tomato paste
2	jalepeño peppers, rinsed, seeded, and diced
½	teaspoon each oregano and comino
¾	cup raisins
¾	cup chopped pimiento
¾	cup sliced, blanched almonds

In a saucepan, crumble the beef and the pork and brown it. Drain off any fat. Add enough water to cover meat. Add the remaining ingredients and simmer *slowly*, stirring occasionally for about an hour or until thick. Serve in a chafing dish with tortilla chips.

Yield: 6 cups

Hot Spinach Dipping Sauce

1	cup chopped onion
1	tablespoon vegetable oil
1	(14½ ounce) can tomato wedges, drained, or 2 tomatoes, peeled, seeded and chopped
1	(10 ounce) package frozen chopped spinach, thawed and squeezed dry
1	tablespoon red wine vinegar
8	ounces cream cheese, softened
2	cups (8 ounces) grated Monterey Jack cheese
1	cup half and half
2	(4 ounce) cans diced green chilies
½	teaspoon comino
	Dash Tabasco or cayenne

In a small skillet cook onions in oil for 5 minutes until they are soft. Stir tomatoes in with onion and cook for a few minutes. Transfer mixture to a bowl and stir in spinach, vinegar, cream cheese, Jack cheese, half and half, chilies, comino, and Tabasco or cayenne. Pour into a buttered ovenproof serving dish and bake at 400° for 15 to 20 minutes until hot and bubbly. Serve with tortilla chips.

Yield: 8 cups

Seafood Dip

Melt all ingredients except the seafood in a double boiler. Do not let the water boil or the mayonnaise will curdle, resulting in an unsightly mess. Fold in the seafood at the last. The dip may be served hot in a chafing dish (again not over direct heat) or at room temperature. It is best when served with Bremner crackers, Carr's, or melba toast, rather than anything too salty.

Yield: 4-5 cups

¾ *cup Hellman's mayonnaise*
1 *tablespoon Dijon-style mustard*
½ *cup white wine*
1 *teaspoon seasoning salt*
  Dash of cayenne
1½ *pounds cream cheese, softened*
1 *pound fresh crabmeat or 1 pound shrimp, coarsely chopped or a combination of both*

Salmon Mousse

Dissolve gelatin in chicken stock over medium heat. Do *not* allow to boil, but be certain that gelatin is all dissolved. Set aside to cool. Drain salmon and remove bones and skin. Mash with a fork. Combine with other ingredients. Pour into a 4 cup mold, rubbed with salad oil or mayonnaise. Cover and chill overnight. To unmold, cut around the edges with a sharp knife and invert onto serving plate lined with red leaf lettuce or Bibb lettuce. If mousse is reluctant to leave the mold, apply warm towels to the top and be patient. Serve with melba toast.

Yield: 4 cups

1 *package unflavored gelatin*
½ *cup chicken stock*
1 *(1 pound) can salmon*
½ *teaspoon dill*
½ *cup minced onion*
⅓ *cup fresh lemon juice*
½ *cup sour cream*
½ *cup cream, whipped*
  Dash Tabasco

Salmon Party Ball

This recipe works well in a Christmas Tree mold. Cover the tree with chopped parsley and decorate with little circles of lemon, orange and apple peel for ornaments. Chopped nuts make wonderful garlands.

1	*(1 pound) can salmon*
1	*(8 ounce) package cream cheese, softened*
2	*tablespoons lemon juice*
1	*teaspoon grated onion*
⅛	*teaspoon horseradish*
¼	*teaspoon salt*
¼	*cup chopped pecans*
¼	*cup snipped parsley*

Drain salmon and remove bones and skin. Combine all ingredients well. Shape into one large ball or two small ones. Roll in pecan/parsley mixture and chill well.

Yield: 1½ cups

Shrimp Mold

I got this recipe from Louise Logan, an old friend and neighbor. The pale pink color of the mold on some Bibb lettuce is so pretty that all you need to do for garnish is tuck a couple of flowers somewhere.

Mix gelatin with warm water. Combine with tomato soup and heat slowly, stirring to dissolve gelatin completely. Do *not* boil. Set aside to cool. Mix cream cheese and mayonnaise. Stir in tomato soup, mixing well. Fold in vegetables and shrimp and add a few drops of Tabasco if desired. Pour into a 6 cup mold, sprayed with Pam or rubbed with salad oil.

Yield: 6 cups

2	**packages unflavored gelatin**
½	**cup warm water**
1	**(10½ ounce) can tomato soup**
1	**(8 ounce) package cream cheese, softened**
1	**cup mayonnaise**
½	**cup minced onion**
½	**cup minced green pepper**
1	**cup minced celery**
12	**ounces cooked shrimp, coarsely chopped**
	Tabasco

Shrimp Butter

1½	*pounds cooked shrimp*
1	*stick butter, softened*
¼	*cup coarsely chopped shallot or*
	green onion
⅛	*teaspoon mace*
½	*teaspoon seasoning salt*
3	*dashes Tabasco*
	Juice of ½ lemon

This recipe is quickly accomplished in a food processor. Coarsely chop half the shrimp, by turning processor on and off. Remove to a bowl. Process remaining ingredients until well blended. Remove from processor and combine with shrimp. Pack into a souffle or other shallow bowl and garnish with a sprig of cilantro or parsley. Serve at room temperature.

Yield: 4 cups

Caviar Pie

My good friend Glenn Whipple was so kind to share this one with me.
Even those who aren't fond of caviar like it.

Grate the boiled egg whites and yolks separately and set aside. Mix cream cheese, mayonnaise, lemon, Worcestershire and Tabasco. Add the white part of the onion. In the glass bowl, make layers in the following order: cream cheese, caviar, egg white, egg yolk. Sprinkle green onion on top of second layer. Serve with melba toast.

Yield: 3 cups

A shallow, glass bowl

2   *boiled eggs*

1   *pound cream cheese, softened*

2-3 *tablespoons Hellman's mayonnaise*

Juice of ½ lemon

Dash Worcestershire

Dash Tabasco

2   *bunches green onions sliced, green tops too (keep separate)*

1   *(4 ounce) jar of caviar, the red is pretty for Christmas*

Cheese and Ripe Olive Spread

1½   (6 ounces) cups Mozzarella
     cheese, grated
½   cup mayonnaise
1   cup sliced ripe olives
½   cup sliced green onion,
     including some green tops

Mix all ingredients. Spread on rye or pumpernickel squares and place under broiler until bubbly. Or serve at room temperature as a spread with crackers or melba toast.

Yield: 2 cups or 16 squares

Gruyère Apple Spread

1   (8 ounce) package cream
     cheese, softened
1   cup (4 ounces) shredded
     Gruyère or Swiss cheese
1   tablespoon milk
2   teaspoons Dijon-style mustard
½   cup peeled, shredded apple
2   tablespoons chopped pecans or
     walnuts
2   teaspoons snipped chives or
     chopped parsley

Mix together cheeses, milk and mustard until blended well. Stir in apples, nuts and parsley or chives. Chill in a serving bowl. Serve at room temperature with crackers, buttered melba toast or pumpernickel squares.

Yield: 2½ cups

Artichoke Squares

Drain artichokes, reserve juice and chop fine, a food processor works well. Sauté onion in enough artichoke marinade to coat the pan. Add cracker crumbs and seasonings to eggs. Stir in cheese, onion and artichokes. Pour into a lightly greased 7 × 11 inch pan and bake at 350° for about 30 minutes. Cool and cut into squares.

Yield: 24-40 squares

2	*(6 ounce) jars marinated artichokes*
½	*cup finely chopped onion*
1	*large garlic clove*
4	*eggs, beaten*
¼	*cup cracker crumbs, crushed*
¼	*teaspoon pepper*
½	*teaspoon oregano*
5	*drops Tabasco*
2	*cups (8 ounces) sharp cheddar cheese, grated*
2	*tablespoons chopped parsley*

TIP: You may use a 9 × 13 inch pan, but reduce baking time by about 10 minutes.

Green Chili Squares

I suppose that we could make squares with most any vegetable by just adding eggs and cheese.

Spray two 9 × 13 inch pans with nonstick spray. Preheat oven to 325°. Mix ingredients well and spread in pans. Bake for 30 minutes or until lightly brown on top. Cool on racks. Cut into squares. These may be frozen on a cookie sheet, then stored in baggies for future use.

Yield: 80 squares

24	*ounces diced green chilies*
10	*ounces grated sharp Cheddar cheese*
10	*ounces grated Monterey Jack cheese*
8	*eggs, beaten*

Spinach and Cheese Squares

4	**cups fresh spinach, lightly packed**
1	**stick butter**
3	**eggs**
1	**cup milk**
1	**cup flour**
½	**teaspoon seasoning salt**
1	**teaspoon baking powder**
1	**pound Monterey Jack cheese, grated**
	Dash Tabasco

Remove stems and wash spinach in a colander. Pat dry with paper towels. Chop lightly by hand or in a food processor. Melt butter in a 9×13 inch pan. Beat eggs. Add milk, flour, salt and baking powder, mixing well. Fold in cheese and spinach. Spread into prepared pan and bake at 350° for 35 minutes. Cool for 30 minutes. Cut into squares. These freeze well.

Yield: 40 squares

Zucchini Squares

Grace Shaffer generously shared this recipe with me when I catered a party for her. It's one of those wonderful "dump and mix" recipes.

3	**cups thinly sliced zucchini**
1	**cup Bisquick**
½	**cup chopped onion**
½	**cup grated Parmesan cheese**
2	**tablespoons chopped parsley**
4	**eggs, beaten**
½	**teaspoon salt**
½	**teaspoon oregano**
¼	**teaspoon garlic powder**
	Pepper
½	**cup vegetable oil**

Mix all ingredients well. Spread into a lightly greased 9×13 inch pan. Bake at 350° for 30 to 40 minutes. Cool for 30 minutes and cut into squares.

Yield: 40 squares

Chicken Liver Pâté

Jacques Pepin is responsible for this wonderful concoction. With a
food processor it is easy to double or triple the recipe for a large party.

1	*pound chicken livers, washed*
⅔	*cup sliced onion*
1	*garlic clove, peeled and crushed*
2	*bay leaves*
¼	*teaspoon thyme leaves*
1	*cup water*
2	*tablespoons salt, divided*
1½	*cups (3 sticks) butter, softened*
	Freshly ground black pepper
2	*teaspoons Cognac*

Place livers, onions, garlic, bay leaves, thyme, water and 1 teaspoon salt in a saucepan. Bring to a boil; reduce heat and simmer for 7 to 8 minutes. Remove from heat and let mixture sit for 5 minutes. Remove solids with a slotted spoon and place in the bowl of a food processor with a metal blade. Reserve stock. Start processing the liver, adding butter piece by piece. Add remaining salt, pepper and Cognac and process for another minute or two. The mixture should be completely smooth. If mixture looks broken down with visible fat, let cool in refrigerator and process again. Pour into a mold.

To decorate the pâté, cut flower petals from cherry tomato skins. Use blanched green onion or parsley stems for the stems. Press your design on top of the pâté. Dissolve a package of unflavored gelatin, 1 cup water and one cup strained liver broth. Stir over medium heat until gelatin is completely dissolved. Place in a pan of ice water to cool slightly. This is the tricky part. If the gelatin gets too cool, of course you can't spoon it over the top of your pâté. If the gelatin is too warm, it will melt the pâté and cause your floral design to float away. If the gelatin becomes congealed, just go back to medium heat and melt it again. This sounds like a lot of trouble and it is, but the end result is quite impressive.

Yield: 2½ cups

Steak Tartar

A tradition in my father's German family was the making of
"Schaferburger." All the chopping of the meat was done with cleavers
on an old butcher block. Of course much singing and beer drinking
accompanied the process as everyone took turns with the cleavers. If
you don't have cleavers a food processor will do.

1	*pound beef round or sirloin, trimmed of all fat and sinew*
¼	*cup minced onion*
1	*teaspoon lemon juice*
½	*teaspoon Worcestershire sauce*
1	*tablespoon capers*
½	*teaspoon anchovy paste*
	Salt
	Lemon pepper

Have your butcher trim the meat carefully so that all you have is meat. *No* fat and *no* sinew! Cut the meat into cubes and grind in a food processor with the steel knife, pulsing several times. Don't overdo this or the meat will be mushy. If you don't have a processor, use a food mill. Or you may have the butcher grind it. Be sure to tell him that you are serving it raw so that it won't be ground after he has ground pork as there is still some danger of trichinosis.

Combine remaining ingredients by hand, just like a meat loaf. Chill overnight. Serve with pumpernickel or as a stuffing for raw mushrooms. You may form it into a mound, ice it with sour cream and sprinkle with capers.

Yield: 10-12 servings

Smoked Turkey Spread

What to do with excess smoked turkey? Remove skin and bones and mince lightly in a food processor. Stir in enough mayonnaise to make a spread. Chopped parsley, chives or cilantro make a nice garnish. Serve with buttered melba toast or crackers.

Marinated Mushrooms

Cut stems from mushrooms. Wash in a colander if they need it. Dry on a paper towel. Combine in container with vinaigrette and parsley and refrigerate. Stir or shake them several times. Let your imagination work with different seasonings for the dressing: dill, Cavender's Greek seasoning, cumin, garlic. I like to add pitted ripe olives for some color.

Yield: 3-4 cups

2	*pints small, fresh mushrooms*
1	*cup vinaigrette dressing*
¼	*cup chopped parsley*

Soy Sauce Marinade

This marinade is wonderful on almost everything, with the possible exception of ice cream sundaes. My mother gave it to me for flank steaks, but we use it on tenderloin, pork chops, hamburger patties, chicken and turkey. Try grilling half a turkey breast; it's great.

½	**cup soy sauce**
2	**tablespoons peanut oil or vegetable oil**
1	**tablespoon honey**
2	**tablespoons vinegar or sherry**
½	**teaspoon ginger powder or fresh ginger, minced**
1	**garlic clove, crushed, or ½ teaspoon garlic powder**
1	**finely chopped green onion**
6	**drops sesame oil, if you like Lemon pepper or just freshly ground pepper**

Pour marinade over meat. This amount covers two flank steaks or equal amounts of other cuts. Marinate for several hours or overnight.

Parmesan Toasts—Gourmet

Bake bread slices at 350° for about 7 to 8 minutes, until just crisp. Rub with garlic, brush generously with olive oil and sprinkle with Parmesan. Return to oven for another 7 to 8 minutes.

Yield: About 20-25 slices

1   long loaf Italian bread, cut into ½ inch slices
1   garlic clove, cut in half crosswise
Olive oil
1   cup freshly grated Parmesan cheese

Melba Toast

I use Pepperidge Farm Thin Sliced White, Wheat, or Multi-Grain bread. You may trim off the crust or not as you desire. Cut bread into halves or quarters. Brush with melted butter. Bake at 300° for 20 to 30 minutes or until golden brown.

Yield: 50 halves

INDEX

INDEX